Growing
Vegetables
year-round

Published by Hyndman Publishing, 325 Purchas Road, RD2, Amberley
ISBN 1-877168-69-6

TEXT & PHOTOGRAPHY: © Dennis Greville
DESIGN & ARTWORK: Dileva Design Ltd.

C O N T E N T S

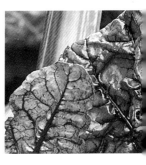

Introduction

Vegetable gardens, whether large or small, can be places of great comfort and satisfaction. It was that great English garden designer, Gertrude Jekyll, who said: "When I want to take a walk for the sheer pleasure of it, I take it amongst the vegetables." Those of us who have strolled through the garden on a hot summer's day, picking a few succulent tomatoes or a handful of peas to munch on as we wander, will surely agree that vegetable gardening is a supremely pleasurable activity. • Freshly dug potatoes or newly picked beans have a beauty all of their own, and sharing this bounty with other members of the family or neighbours is a special way in which all of us can benefit and further enjoy the fruits of our labour. • Growing your own vegetables and herbs is also a good way to ensure that what you are eating is not only spray free, but also grown organically. Although some may argue that it is cheaper and easier to buy vegetables from the supermarket or a commercial grower, the

Flowers and vegies mixed in a potager garden: black palm tree cabbage (cavolo nero palmizio), red silver beet (beta vulgaris), mimulus, orache (atriplex hortensis) and chicory.

Pot with vegies.

Nihil est agricultura melius nihil uberius
Nihil dulcius nihil homine libero dignius

"Nothing is better, more fruitful, more pleasant,
And more worthy of a free man, than agriculture."

Cicero (106 BC–43 BC), from *De officiis* (On Duties) I. 151

committed gardener and cook will insist that fresh, vital and unadulterated produce is the most important ingredient in the production of healthy and delicious meals. • For the most part our New Zealand soils are naturally fertile and the climate will allow us to grow something edible for almost the entire growing season. Water can be a precious commodity in some areas and winter cold a problem in others, but with a little thought and organisation most problems can be overcome. • For those living in the country where space isn't at a premium, a vegetable garden may mean a large, intensively worked plot. For city dwellers a simple potager where flowers and vegetables are cleverly worked together may be all that is possible. Whatever the size of your vegetable garden, the simple pleasures of growing and eating your own produce are guaranteed to delight people of all ages and lifestyles.

Larger vegetable garden.

The Productive Vegetable Garden

Organic or Inorganic?

Organic gardening has increased in popularity in recent years, as many keen gardeners have turned away from the idea of a short-term fix and are taking a more sustainable approach. Committed organic gardeners believe that the constant use of chemicals will result in poorer and poorer yields, while at the same time filling the environment with harmful chemicals. Many organic gardeners will also tell you that chemical-free crops have more flavour.

Organic gardening requires a little extra patience and hard work, but it is possible to establish a healthy garden without resorting to chemical fertilisers, treatments and sprays. For those who wish to 'go organic', here are some suggestions to bear in mind when establishing your garden.

Organic Fertilisers

Committed organic gardeners prefer to use only those fertilisers that contain natural products (such as fish manure or emulsion, chicken manure, dried blood, blood and bone, and even processed seaweed). These fertilisers will certainly help plants access the food they need, but remember that organic fertilisers will not work until the micro-organisms that live in the soil have broken them down. When the weather is warm the micro-organisms are more active, but if the soil is wet and cold their action will be greatly reduced. The smaller the particles, the quicker the nutrients can be released, so during the winter months choose finely ground organic fertilisers (such as dried blood).

Make your own compost with kitchen and garden waste.

Organic Disease & Pest Control

Organic methods may be slower and less complete than chemical solutions, but in the long run they are safer for us and better for the environment. Regular watering and feeding will go a long way towards ensuring disease-free crops and flowers. Plants that are well fed (not overfed) and not stressed will better resist diseases.

As for insect pests, small infestations don't have the organic gardener running to use powerful pesticides; rather they can be contained and suffered, especially if crops are healthy. 'Nature's Way' sprays and other organic pest control products can be used without fear on edible crops. They have a very low toxicity and a withholding period is not required. (Chemical pest control sprays usually have a withholding period, which means that after using these sprays you must wait a set time before it is safe to eat treated crops.)

Most of us will admit to using a mix of both organic and inorganic gardening techniques, and both methods are discussed in this book. Choose the solutions that best suit your garden (and your conscience!)

Soil

Acid and Alkaline Soils

The kind of plants that you can grow will depend on the amount of calcium or lime in your soil. These elements both affect the availability of nutrients to the plant roots. Soil acidity is gauged on the pH scale, which measures from 1 (extremely acid) to 14 (extremely alkaline). A pH of 7 is neutral and suits the growing of most vegetables.

Some plants prefer a limey alkaline soil, while others like an acid one. To make a soil alkaline add dolomite or ground limestone. To make a soil more acid add sulphate of ammonia or flowers of sulphur in the quantities recommended by the manufacturer.

General Soil Care

The best garden soil consists of lots of well-made compost, mixed with organic material such as sheep or horse manure, and reinforced with a general garden fertiliser with a nitrogen / phosphorus / potassium ratio of 6 / 5 / 5 (with trace elements added).

All soils will benefit from the addition of plenty of compost or well-rotted manure. Mulching your soil regularly with whatever organic materials you have available will greatly improve its quality. Sawdust, seaweed, coffee grounds, spent hops, bark, grass clippings, and compost will rot down quickly to create valuable humus.

Dolomite lime or lime proper both have the effect of neutralising or reducing the acidity of the soil. Lime encourages soil bacteria and earthworms and these all combine to break down organic matter while at the same time providing nutrients for plants. Spread lime or dolomite evenly, and fork it in or leave the task to the rain. After three weeks, add a general-purpose fertiliser, blood and bone, or layers of compost.

Green Manure Crops

Green manure crops have long been used to add organic material and nitrogen to the soil. Traditionally, alfalfa, barley, lupin, peas, oats, mustard and rape have been used to this end. Mustard will do better in the warmer north, while lupin and oats are better where the weather is colder. Alfalfa has roots that penetrate deeply, breaking up heavy, compacted soil. Sow them early in the autumn and dig the crop in as soon as it begins flowering. If green crops are left too long they become tough and difficult to dig in. Cover the crop with a few centimetres of soil and speed up the process of decomposition by sprinkling over a little sulphate of ammonia, nitrate of soda or dried blood.

Soil Types

Different soil types present different challenges to the gardener. Identifying the type of soil which is predominant in your garden will enable you to administer the most appropriate remedies.

Probe meters and liquid soil pH testers are available from most garden centres. They will tell you whether your soil is acid or alkaline. Laboratory tests are more accurate and may be available from your friendly local laboratory.

Well-rotted animal manure makes a valuable addition to the vegetable garden.

To identify your soil type, pick up a handful of damp soil and rub it in your hand:

- If it feels gritty and is difficult to roll into a ball, it's sandy.
- If it feels gritty but can be rolled into a ball, it's loam.
- If it feels sticky but can be rolled into a ball, it's clay loam.
- If you can stretch and roll the ball into a cylinder, it's clay and probably more suitable for potting rather than gardening!

Sandy

Sandy soils are very free draining and dry out quickly in the summer. It can be difficult to prevent moisture and nutrients from leaching out of this loose soil.

- By adding plenty of compost to such a soil, moisture and nutrients can be retained and made use of by your plants.
- Mulching a light, sandy soil also helps retain moisture. Add layers of newspaper as mulch, or incorporate either sawdust or compost into the sand. In fact, you can use any material that will hold moisture.
- A surface mulch of grass clippings, sawdust or even shingle can help conserve moisture and make sandy soils more productive.

Loam

Loam soils are every gardener's dream. They are rich and moderately free draining. They can be improved by the addition of compost and light mulch before summer arrives.

Clay Loam

Clay loams are easier to break up than pure clay soils. Compost and regular additions of sand as well as lime or dolomite will quickly produce a good productive soil.

Clay

Clay soil presents the biggest problem for the gardener. It can become a solid lump in the summer and a soggy swamp in the winter, and plants are difficult to start in clay soils, especially during a wet spring. But these difficulties are not insurmountable, and there are numerous techniques which can be used to improve clay soil.

- Clay soils will improve greatly if you can drain them. If the soil is low lying and wet, it may be necessary to dig trenches and lay drains in order to raise the beds above the soil surface (see *Raised Beds* section following).
- Dig and break up clay soils in the spring when they are beginning to dry out. The time to do this is limited as these types of soils change quickly from very soft to hard in a matter of weeks. Digging clay soils in the winter is likely to do more harm than good.
- Clay can also be broken up by the addition of plenty of organic material. Use animal manure if available, or try clay improvers such as gypsum, rotted pea straw, sand, sawdust, compost, coffee grounds, perlite and peat. These will eventually break up very heavy soils.

Adding gypsum...

sawdust...

compost...

and sand.

Adding lime can also help to open up, or flocculate, the clay particles, thus making it easier for water to pass through. (Note: Add these materials as the soil warms in the spring. Adding manure to cold clay soil will result in the formation of toxic compounds that will only poison your plants.)

- Clay soil can be warmed up and dried out by covering with large sheets of plastic or you can also plant under cloches. Once warmed up, clay soils hold their heat longer than sandy ones.

Raised Beds

Raised garden beds are another way of coping with troublesome soil. By building up a frame of wood, railway sleepers, brick or stone, a raised bed can be created relatively easily.

After building the edge of your raised bed you need to fill it with friable, rich soil. The best way to do this is to dig and remove the soil from one end of the bed and slowly mix it with as much organic material as you can lay your hands on. Disease and weed-free garden waste, newspaper and untreated sawdust can also be placed at the bottom of the bed. Little by little the bed can be built up and levelled. You can add fertiliser such as blood and bone as you proceed. Adding lime can also help with the drainage of wet soils.

Raised beds are a boon for gardeners in areas where the weather is wet and the soil needs draining.

Fertilisers

Feeding the garden makes a big difference, as it affects how quickly plants can access the food they need. Before using fertilisers to address more specific concerns, it pays to ensure that your garden has the three basic nutrients required for healthy, balanced plant growth: nitrogen (N), phosphorus (P) and potassium (K).

The combination of these three elements in a fertiliser is referred to as the NPK balance. It is commonly displayed on the packets of most commercially available products and tells you precisely how much of each nutrient there is in any particular mix. Each of the three nutrients plays a different role in plant growth, but no plant will grow and mature properly without a combination of these elements.

Nitrogen

Nitrogen helps to develop stems and leaves. Nitrogen can either be supplied by using a general artificial fertiliser (which contains a mix of nitrogen, phosphorus and potassium), or by using an organic product. Weak plants will respond quickly to small additions of any nitrogenous material, whether organic or inorganic.

Inorganic sources of nitrogen

- Nitrate of soda – 16% nitrogen content
- Sulphate of ammonia – 20%
- Urea – 40% (use sparingly or water down to prevent burning soft plant tissue)

Organic sources of nitrogen

- Bonedust – 4%
- Blood and bone – 6%
- Fish manure – 7%
- Dried blood – 10% (very gentle in action and quickly absorbed; an excellent food for top dressing small plants)

Dried blood.

Phosphorus

Phosphorus encourages flowering and ripening, stimulates root development and helps plants to withstand drought.

Inorganic sources of phosphorus

- Superphosphate – 100% (contains no nitrogen or potassium)

Organic sources of phosphorus

- Blood and bone – 7% (blood & bone contains no potassium)

Blood and bone.

Potassium

Potassium stimulates the production of starch and sugars, as well as healthy growth, better colour, flowering and fruiting in plants. It encourages root crops in particular such as potatoes.

Inorganic sources of potassium

- Sulphate of potash - 48% pure potash (contains no nitrogen or phosphorus, but is an important ingredient in any balanced inorganic fertiliser mix). Sulphate of potash improves the quality of leaf crops, fruit and flowers. It encourages dark green healthy growth and strengthens plants against disease. Apply at a rate of 1–2 handfuls per square metre.

Organic sources of potassium

- Rock potash
- Wood ash

Trace Elements

Copper, zinc, iron, manganese, boron and molybdenum are also necessary to the production of healthy crops. These elements may or may not be present in your soil. Soil which has been cropped for a long time and fertilised with animal manure will generally be lacking in these important ingredients. Trace elements can be purchased in a mix and added to your soil in small quantities. Many balanced fertilisers also contain trace elements.

Lime and Dolomite Lime

Lime encourages soil bacteria and the activity of earthworms. It also helps break up heavy soil and acts as a release agent for dormant plant foods. It is an essential ingredient for the healthy garden. Ground limestone or calcium carbonate is often sold containing trace minerals.

Some gardeners prefer dolomite lime, which is a mixture of calcium and magnesium carbonate. Apply at a quantity of a handful per square metre at least three weeks before applying other organic or inorganic fertilisers.

Aluminium Sulphate

Aluminium sulphate is used to acidify the soil and helps produce healthy and sweet potatoes, radishes and tomatoes. It can be mixed in water and applied when the plants are growing vigorously or sprinkled on the soil in spring and summer.

Slow Release Fertilisers

There are now many slow release fertilisers available on the market. They contain all the major elements necessary for healthy plant growth and release them slowly over a period of months. Slow release products feed your plants when they need it and cannot cause fertiliser burn. Some slow release fertilisers are affected by the temperature of the soil - check this factor before applying them to cold winter soils. Slow release fertilisers are ideal for light, sandy soils.

Sample slow release fertiliser:

- Nitrophoska – slow release fertiliser that works best in the warmer weather. Apply in the recommended quantities.

Long-term Slow Release Fertilisers

These products will release food to your plants over a two year period. They are ideal in helping to establish healthy, vigorous growth. Many can be used at planting time and added to the soil or scattered at the base of your plants.

Sample long-term slow release fertiliser:

- Magamp – long-term slow release fertiliser which works over two years. Apply in the recommended quantities for vegetables in containers. (For small containers apply 60 g; for large containers apply 240 g.)

Tips for Applying Fertilisers

- Make sure you follow the manufacturer's instructions. Too much fertiliser can burn and limit the plant's growth. Too little will prevent the plant growing to its potential.
- Apply carefully. If you are applying a dry fertiliser when the plant's leaves are wet, make sure that you water it in well.
- High nitrogen fertilisers are the most likely to damage young roots and burn leaves – take extra care with these.
- Always apply a little at a time.
- Fertiliser applied before sowing or planting should be worked into the soil well – this should be done several weeks beforehand. Apply

When tending your garden, don't forget the humble compost heap. Compost is an invaluable soil conditioner and when mixed with other organic or inorganic fertiliser it greatly improves the production of the garden.

Adding aluminium sulphate to water.

A simple compost bin can be made from a coil of chicken wire. This is all that is needed to contain organic matter as it breaks down into compost.

more fertiliser once the plants are growing vigorously.

- Sprinkle fertiliser on top of the soil, but don't put it where it can come into direct contact with tender young roots.

Making Your Own Fertilisers

Liquid fertilisers sprayed on leaves, fruits and flowers will produce quick and satisfying results. Food applied in a liquid form is instantly available to the plants, which means stronger, healthier plants and tastier, heavier vegetable crops.

Simple liquid fertilisers cost nothing and are easy to prepare. They can be made from fish waste, bird, cow, horse and pig manure, and seaweed, as well as various herbs and nettles. Even grass clippings can be made into useful liquid manure for the garden.

The simplest way to make your own liquid fertiliser is to place these materials in a watering can, soaking the waste for at least a week before diluting it and watering onto the garden. You may need to strain thicker liquid fertilisers to prevent them blocking the watering can or sprayer. Grass clipping fertiliser can be applied without diluting it.

If you decide on the bulk approach, leave a large bag of fish waste or several shovelfuls of manure to soak for a week in a large 200 litre container of water, then dilute one part of this brew to three parts of water. The resulting liquid can then be sprayed onto the leaves or watered onto the roots to produce quick growing, healthy plants. This soaking process can be repeated several times with the same manure before it is depleted of nutrients. Tanks or a drum system (either fitted with a tap or without) can be useful if you want to produce large quantities.

Grass clippings or fish scraps placed in water for several weeks will produce a valuable and quick acting liquid fertiliser.

To keep liquid fertilisers from burning roots and leaves always apply to moist soil and wet leaves and avoid use in the heat of the day. The results of liquid fertiliser will begin to show in the garden within a few weeks. Quick growing plants such as lettuce will respond almost immediately to liquid food and you'll probably notice the difference within days.

Biodynamic Liquid Fertiliser

This famous liquid fertiliser consists of six herbs: stinging nettle, chamomile, dandelion, oak tree bark (or oak leaves), yarrow (achillea), and valerian (valerian officinalis). Each of these herbs helps to activate the organisms that live in the soil. They also speed up the fermentation of compost and manure, making them more suitable for the garden.

To make true biodynamic liquid fertiliser use equal proportions of each herb. Using just one or two and applying the liquid to the soil will also have beneficial results. Valerian tea is said to attract earthworms. Nettle and dandelion will stimulate healthy vigorous growth. The herbs can be added to water and allowed to rot down before being applied to the garden, or brought to the boil and allowed to cool.

Beneficial garden teas

Herb and other garden teas are cheap and simple to make, and will improve the health and vigour of the garden. Teas are an ideal way to transfer beneficial essences from one plant to another.

If you are using herbs, cut them early in the morning and before they have flowered. That way the beneficial influences are at their peak. Dry herbs in the shade and store in paper bags until they are needed.

When needed cover the herbs with water and bring to the boil. Remove from the heat and cool for at least 20 minutes. You can use the tea directly on your plants or dilute it with 3 parts of water. Use immediately after preparation, as the beneficial properties won't last.

Here are some beneficial garden teas made from herbs and other organic materials:

- **Nettle tea** – Rich in iron. If nettle tea is sprayed onto plants they will be strengthened and better able to withstand drought. Try growing basil and tomato plants together and watering with nettle tea for best results.

- **Chamomile tea** – Apply to the roots of flowers, trees, shrubs and vegetables when planting.

- **St John's wort tea** (hypericum) – Apply to the roots of flowers, trees, shrubs and vegetables when planting.

- **Dandelion tea** – This plant exudes a substance that inhibits the growth of neighbouring plants. However, when it is made into a herb tea or used in the compost it has a beneficial influence on plant growth.

- **Sage tea** – Great growth stimulant for established plants.

- **Grass clipping tea** – Steeped in water for several weeks, this makes an ideal fertiliser for encouraging growth in tomatoes and many other plants.

- **Worm tea** – If you have a worm farm, pour the occasional bucket of water over it and collect the residue, as it will be rich in minerals. This worm tea can then be used at full strength or diluted (dilute one part of worm tea with three parts of water) when planting young seedlings. It can also be watered on to pot plants.

- **Manure tea** – Soak a bag containing horse or cow manure in a bucket or a 190 litre (44 gallon) drum. (Proportions should be roughly one part of manure to three parts of water.) Leave for 24 hours. The resulting brew will be either dark black or brown depending on the concentration. Dilute it even further until it is the colour of weak tea. Water onto young seedlings when planting or pour the solution onto the ground around established plants for quick results. Apply manure tea with a watering can.

Watering the garden.

Sizing Up Your Options

Courtyard Containers

Even the smallest courtyard can support a selection of salad crops and vegetables. However, if you want to get the best from container plants, you'll need to take a little extra care with both their planting and maintenance.

Here are a few things to keep in mind when planning a container garden:

- Choose vegetables which are well suited to container gardening. Climbing beans, lettuce, parsley, dill, beetroot, spring onion and mint are ideal.
- Garden soil should not be used in a container as it is too heavy and doesn't drain well. Use a potting mix that is lightly fertilised.
- Consider using a moisture-retaining material. Crystal rain and other such products can be added dry to your soil mix at a rate of one teaspoon to five litres of soil. These crystals absorb moisture and help to extend the time necessary between watering. They also guarantee healthier, less stressed plants. (For plants which are already established, you can easily make a few holes in the soil with a pencil and drop in a sprinkling of crystals.) Water well after adding the crystals to the soil.
- 'Wettasoil' and other wetting agents are a real boon for the container vegetable gardener. Simply add 15 ml to a nine litre watering can and water your plants. The water will go right to the bottom of the pot, considerably extending the time between watering. This will save you both time and money and ensure vigorous and healthy plants.
- Sunlight is essential for healthy plants. If your containers are in half light, be sure to turn them regularly to ensure even growth. Pots on bases with wheels or rollers are especially useful as they are easy to move.

Vegetable Patches

A larger vegetable garden requires a lot of thought and planning if it is to be successful. Here are a few things to bear in mind when planning a larger vegetable garden:

- Determine your requirements first. You may wish to concentrate on crops that are easy to grow (like onions, silver beet and radishes); crops which are expensive at certain times of the year (such as new

Climbing beans, lettuce, parsley, dill, beetroot, spring onions and mint all growing happily together in containers in a small city courtyard.

'Wettasoil' is a useful deep watering agent especially suitable for container gardening.

Potager Gardening

While the most common form of potager gardening is to dot flowers amongst the vegetables, it is also possible to plant cabbages between the shrubs and perennials and onions in the rose beds. A clump of coloured silver beet in a pot at the front door can be just as appealing and considerably more useful than a cyclamen or a row of marigolds.

Large vegetable gardens require careful planning.

potatoes); crops which are best eaten fresh from the garden (like peas, globe artichokes and sweet corn); crops which can be stored easily (like carrots and beans); or crops which give a long harvest (like Brussels sprouts and spinach).

- The most important requirement for any vegetable garden, large or small, is sunlight. Most vegetables require at least 6 hours of sunlight per day, although leafy vegetables like chicory, lettuce and spinach will grow in 4 - 6 hours of sunlight.
- Air circulation, shade from tall trees, shelter from strong winds and drainage also need careful consideration.
- In large gardens rows need to be spaced far enough apart to allow for easy access, carrying of equipment, cultivation and harvesting. In smaller gardens permanent paths can provide access to the plants.
- To reduce garden maintenance try a black plastic cover - this will limit weed growth and hasten the development of crops by warming the soil, while at the same time helping to conserve moisture. You will need to make holes in the plastic to plant your crops, and you may also need to make more holes in the plastic for watering in summer. It also pays to put slug and snail bait under the plastic as you lay it to prevent colonies of these pests developing.
- Unless you want the whole crop at once, sow at intervals to stagger the harvest. Be aware that some crops (like cabbages and Brussels sprouts) can last for a long time in the garden without spoiling.

Inter-cropping

Inter-cropping is used to get as many vegetables out of a piece of land as possible. These plants can be sown and then harvested between slower growing crops: beetroot, carrot, Chinese cabbage, corn salad, lettuce, radish, spinach, spring onion and turnip. Sweet corn has little foliage and can also be inter-cropped with low leafy vegetables such as lettuce and chicory.

Growing from Seed

Saving Seeds

Seeds saved from vegetable crops are a thrifty and independent way to replenish your garden.

- Just what seeds to save is an important consideration. A general rule is to steer clear of hybrid plants, as many will not come true to type from seed.
- When they are ripe, seed heads usually turn brown or black, dry out and start to split.
- Bean seeds are perhaps the easiest to collect. They are large and store well. By observing when the first seeds begin to fall, you will know when they are ready to collect. You need to get to them when they are still dry and unaffected by the rain.
- Paper bags are excellent for storing seeds in. They can be hung up in an airy, shady place to dry for at least a week. Seeds that become too hot, cold or damp after collecting will not germinate well.
- Never use plastic bags or sealed plastic containers to store your seeds, as the presence of even the smallest amount of moisture will encourage fungal infections.
- When storing seeds, the paper bag must be clean of any insects, leaves and bits of seed capsule. These can introduce diseases when the new seedlings are grown.

- A sieve is useful when cleaning seed. Shake the sieve containing your collected seed over a sheet of white paper. You will quickly be able to identify any insect pests and be able to remove them and any debris.
- Pour the clean seed into labelled envelopes. A teaspoon of silica gel (cobalt chloride) from the chemist will keep seed dry. Place the gel in small cloth bags before adding to the envelopes.

Saving bean and cabbage seeds is easy. Choose the healthiest, longest and most regular pods and store the seed carefully until next spring.

Hardening Off & After Care

- Seedlings should be gradually introduced to cooler outside temperatures. Having been raised in a protected environment, they will quickly succumb to cold winds unless they are introduced to the garden gradually.
- Slugs, snails and birds will also be a threat to new plants. Use a suitable bait and, if necessary, cover your seedlings with chicken wire until they are well established.
- Place seedlings in filtered rather than direct sunlight to start with.
- Water sparingly with a liquid feed mixed with a fungicide to boost plant growth.
- When your plants are growing strongly plant them out into ground that has been well prepared.

Sowing Seeds

As long as seeds are sown in a sterile, moist, warm seed-raising mix, there is little that can go wrong. By also providing protection from digging cats, foraging birds and predatory slugs and snails, success is almost guaranteed.

Firm the soil and water it well before sowing.

Using a folded piece of paper will make sowing seed easier. Cover lightly with soil once sown and water again.

Pricking out – seedlings pricked out into a pot.

What Can Go Wrong?

Rotted Seed

- This problem is caused by fungi that kill germinating seeds. You can take steps to prevent seeds rotting by using only good quality, sterilised soil when you are sowing seed.
- You can also minimise seed failure by sowing only when the soil is warm, as cold soils will cause many seeds to rot. A seed propagator with heating pad can help get around this problem. A basic propagating unit that includes a heat pad is not that expensive.
- Over-watering can also cause seeds to rot. Once the seeds have been well watered for the first time, it pays to use a misting bottle to water until the seeds germinate. This way water is kept to a minimum. Another effective way of watering is simply to stand the tray in a shallow bath of water so that moisture percolates from the bottom of the tray up. Do not fill the bath with so much water that it overflows the rim of the tray onto the seeds and the compost. After the soil is moist stand the tray out to drain.

Seedlings ready for planting out. Disturb the root system as little as possible and plant into well prepared soil.

Damping Off Disease

This disease can strike any young seedlings. The young stems wither away at soil level, seedlings topple over, and then die in circular patches. To prevent damping off and ensure healthy seeds:

- Firm the soil first and water it well before sowing.
- Sow seed thinly.
- Use good quality seed raising mixes that contain an anti-damping off agent.
- Always use fresh seed raising mix. Don't be tempted to use mix that has grown other plants.
- Dispose of affected seedlings at the first sign of disease and water any healthy remaining seedlings with 'Thiram' or a similar fungicide.

Punnets of ready grown mixed salad and other vegetable plants are readily available at most garden centres. Buying them already half grown can save a lot of time and work.

Companion Planting

Plants growing together will interact with one another, particularly within the confines of a small vegetable patch. For example, a tall-growing species will provide much needed cover for shade-loving plants, but may suppress other low-growing sun loving plants. Many plants release excretions into the soil through both their leaves and roots - some plants find these excretions toxic, while others thrive in such an environment. Plants can also interact by competing for food or water. By carefully choosing those plants which grow well together, you will enjoy better flowering, heavier crops and a more bountiful garden.

Planting lettuce and French marigolds (tagetes patula) together.

Examples of Beneficial Companion Planting

Sweet basil, parsley & tomato

The highly aromatic nature of sweet basil and parsley makes these plants great companions for many vegetable crops, particularly tomatoes. A rich moist soil suits them all. Try growing basil and parsley together and watering with nettle tea for best results.

Marigold, lettuce, strawberries & tomatoes

The French marigold (tagetes patula) excretes a substance into the soil that limits the spread of harmful soil nematodes. It is especially beneficial when grown with lettuce, strawberries and tomatoes.

Rosemary, sage & cabbages

Rosemary and sage will flourish when planted together. Sage tea is an ideal growth stimulant for established plants. Sage is a perfect companion plant for cabbage.

Corn, pumpkins & beans

Corn, pumpkins and beans are wonderful neighbours. Early planted corn gives shelter and provides a structure for beans to climb on. Pumpkins benefit from the shade provided by these taller-growing neighbours.

Silver beet & lavender

Silver beet and lavender grow well together. Lavender is a useful plant to have in the garden, as it attracts bees and raises the level of beneficial aromas in the garden.

Dill & corn

Dill also attracts bees into the garden. A row of dill on either side of a patch of corn makes both plants grow stronger and bear more heavily.

Pumpkins and beans.

Foxglove (digitalis purpurea).

Onions, garlic & parsley

Onions, garlic and parsley make ideal companion plants. Parsley also grows well with roses and tomatoes. Parsley attracts bees into the garden when it flowers.

Broccoli, potato, radishes & nasturtiums

Nasturtiums planted near broccoli will keep aphids away. Nasturtiums also benefit potatoes and radishes. Nasturtium makes an excellent herb tea for both spraying as well as watering onto plants.

Foxglove (digitalis)

Foxglove has a growth stimulating effect on all the plants growing near it. It is said to protect the garden from disease and strengthen tender plants. Useful and decorative, the foxglove can be grown in both the vegetable and flower garden.

Attracting Bees to the Garden

Most vegetable plants have inconspicuous flowers which don't attract valuable pollinating bees. By placing a hive in the vegetable garden or planting bee-attracting flowers such as borage, thyme, catnip, sweet basil or mint, your vegetable yield will be substantially increased.

Attract bees by placing a hive in the vegetable garden.

Borage (borage officinalis), a favourite of the bees.

Easy to Grow Vegetables

Asparagus
(Asparagus Officinalis)

GROWING TIMES
Asparagus are perennial plants that will produce regularly for over 20 years. The edible aerial stem 'spears' appear each spring.

HEIGHT / SPREAD
Height 1–1.5 metres when flowering. Give asparagus 30–50 cm between each plant, and space rows 1.2 metres apart.

FROST HARDINESS
Very frost hardy.

SUN, SOIL, WATER, FOOD
A position in full sun is essential. Add plenty of compost and animal manure to the soil, plus a complete fertiliser (NPK 10 / 4 / 6). Add a little lime if the soil is acidic. The chosen bed must be dug deeply and the soil well broken up. River sand added to the soil will help provide good drainage. Asparagus suck a lot of nourishment from the ground.

FLOWERS
Asparagus flower profusely and set large crops of seed. Sow seeds in spring. Asparagus produce both male and female plants. Male plants bear better spears so it is a good idea to discard the females once they have set seed. The females are easily distinguished as they produce seed in the second autumn after sowing.

GROWING FROM CUTTINGS OR SEED
Asparagus can be grown from seed, but this process takes time. The more usual method is to plant 2 year old crowns. Once the beds are prepared and the new crowns planted, they will continue to produce for 20 years or more.

CARE / MAINTENANCE
At the end of the autumn the ferny foliage will turn yellow and die back. This foliage can be burnt where it falls, the ash returned to the soil and the beds top dressed with compost and a general fertiliser. In winter cut plants to ground level and lightly cultivate the soil.

PLANTING

Plant two year old crowns as they will bear more quickly. These can be purchased from most garden centres. Do not harvest the young shoots or spears until the third spring so as to allow the crowns to mature. If white asparagus spears are preferred, cut well below the soil just as they break the surface. 'Martha Washington' is a well known variety that produces long, thick spears. The newer F1 hybrids (such as 'Gourmet Purple') also produce thick spears and are high yielding.

HARVESTING

In the third year after planting limit the cutting of spears to between four and six weeks. In the following year the cutting time can be extended to six or even ten weeks if the plants are growing well. Cut when the spears are 20–25 cm long, taking care not to cut forming spears that are still under the ground.

PESTS AND DISEASES

Asparagus are generally disease free.

IN POTS AND TUBS

Asparagus can be grown in pots and tubs for decoration. The fine fern-like foliage is very attractive. For generous crops they are better planted in beds.

Aubergine (Eggplant)

(Solanum Melongena)

GROWING TIMES

Aubergines grow best where the summer season is hot and long. Sow seeds in August under glass for planting out as soon as the soil warms. In temperate parts of the country plant in a glass house.

HEIGHT / SPREAD

1 m x 50 cm.

FROST HARDINESS

Frost tender.

SUN, SOIL, WATER, FOOD

They do best in a uniformly moist but well-drained soil that is rich in organic material. Potash and liquid fertiliser will also help boost growth. Nip out the top of each plant when they get to 15–20 cm high and restrict the branches to three or four.

FLOWERS

Pollination can be a problem, as bees are not overly attracted to the aubergine flower. This can be remedied by hand pollinating with a soft water colour paintbrush or by planting bee-attracting flowers nearby.

GROWING FROM CUTTINGS OR SEED

Sow a clump of seeds in a small pot as early as possible because the eggplant needs a long season to mature. When they are large enough to handle, prick out seedlings and place into individual pots. Give plenty of liquid fertiliser and plant out only when the weather is warm.

CARE / MAINTENANCE
Ripen 5–6 fruits to each plant, pinching out any further flowers that might appear.

PLANTING
Plant 5–6 plants for a family of four.

HARVESTING
Harvest when the skin is a glowing, rich, even purple. Never wait until the eggplant starts to lose its glossy shine, as it will be too tough for good eating and the seeds become bitter in over-ripe fruit.

PESTS AND DISEASES
Wilt often attacks the eggplant. This soil borne fungal disease is difficult to cure. At the first sign of plant failure remove and burn (or otherwise dispose of) all parts of the plant. If several plants are affected refrain from growing any members of the solanum (tomato, potato, capsicum) family in the same area for at least two years.

IN POTS AND TUBS
Available in many shapes and sizes, the eggplant makes an attractive and unusual container plant. They are also available in white, pink, purple or purple-black, depending on the variety.

Beans
– French Bean, Kidney Bean, String Bean & Haricot Bean (Phaseolus Vulgaris)

GROWING TIMES
Beans need warm soil to be grown successfully. October and November are the best months in which to sow seed. In the coldest parts of the south it is worth waiting until late November or early December.

HEIGHT / SPREAD
Originally a climber, many dwarf beans have now been developed from phaseolus vulgaris. Pods vary in length. Some are round, while others are flat. They vary in colour from cream to yellow, green, blue-green, red or purple. The seed colours and markings also vary considerably. 'Blue Lake' (pictured opposite) is a tall climber that bears plump, long, tender, bluish-green pods. 'Gourmet's Delight' and 'Purple Tee Pee' are dwarf forms, growing to no more than 50 cm. 'Hestia' is an early dwarf bean which grows to 50 cm. It has been specially developed for container growing. The attractive red and white flowers are followed by dark green stringless beans.

FROST HARDINESS
Not frost hardy.

SUN, SOIL, WATER, FOOD
Beans enjoy well-rotted compost, good drainage and a sunny position. Make sure you provide adequate moisture, especially after the first set of flowers.

FLOWERS
Wetting the foliage when the plants are flowering helps create a humid, moist atmosphere that is favourable for pollination. Regular picking also encourages flowering.

GROWING FROM CUTTINGS OR SEED
Dust seeds with fungicide before planting. Soil should be moist and well-drained but not wet. Do not soak bean seeds overnight as it will only encourage them to rot. Sow seeds in rows 50–60 cm apart. Plant them 5 cm deep and 10 cm apart. Choose an open sunny site, preferably with the rows running east to west.

CARE / MAINTENANCE
Train tall growing varieties on poles or between wires. Provide dwarf varieties with the support of brush or bamboo, or train between string lines.

PLANTING

A 5 m row will produce a good quantity of beans. Sow a second crop as soon as your seedlings begin to develop their distinctive mature bean leaves.

HARVESTING

Pick all beans (dwarf or climbing) when they are tender. Regular watering and picking will keep them producing for several months.

PESTS AND DISEASES

Aphids, green vegetable bugs (shield beetles), caterpillars, red spidermite, rust and white fly will all undermine the health and vigour of your beans. Treat with chemical or natural remedies at the first sign of damage.

IN POTS AND TUBS

Dwarf varieties such as 'Hestia' are very suitable for container gardening.

Beans

— Runner (Phaseolus Coccineus)

GROWING TIMES

Summer and autumn.

HEIGHT / SPREAD

3 m x 1 m.

FROST HARDINESS

Perennial and moderately frost hardy.

SUN, SOIL, WATER, FOOD

Runner beans enjoy well-rotted compost, good drainage and a sunny position. Make sure you provide adequate moisture, especially after the first set of flowers. They can be perennial if the soil is well drained and warm throughout the winter. The large tap roots will spring back into growth each season for several years but eventually lose their vigour. When the soil has warmed you can sow the seeds 30 cm apart and 5 cm deep. A double row grown on both sides of an open trellis or wire fence is best.

All beans are easily damaged if they are planted in windy, exposed conditions.

FLOWERS

Both red and white flowering varieties are available.

GROWING FROM CUTTINGS OR SEED

Dust seeds with fungicide (or dip) before planting. Soil should be moist and well-drained but not wet. Do not soak bean seeds overnight as it will only encourage them to rot. Sow seeds in rows 50–60 cm apart. Plant them 5 cm deep and 10 cm apart. Choose an open sunny site, preferably with the rows running east to west.

CARE / MAINTENANCE

Train up bamboo poles and stakes or grow to cover warm walls and trellis.

PLANTING

Plant in warm, moist, well drained soil in a sheltered part of the garden.

HARVESTING

Pick when young and tender. Dense foliage may hide beans and they quickly become tough and not worth picking. Leave some to mature and dry to start fresh plants next season.

PESTS AND DISEASES

Aphids, green vegetable bugs (shield beetles), caterpillars, red spidermite, rust and white fly will all undermine the health and vigour of your beans. Treat with chemical or natural remedies at the first sign of damage.

IN POTS AND TUBS

Constant moisture is essential for the growing of tender runner beans. They will grow happily up bamboo poles placed in pots and containers, as long as the soil is moist and rich and the position sunny. The brilliant red flowers are very attractive.

Beetroot

(Beta Vulgaris)

GROWING TIMES

Sow seeds outdoors from mid spring through to early autumn for harvesting in 65–70 days when the roots are 5–7.5 cm. Seed sown in late autumn or winter sometimes runs to seed. In warm, frost free parts of the country seeds can be sown at almost any time.

HEIGHT / SPREAD

40–45 cm x 10 cm.

FROST HARDINESS

Generally frost hardy.

SUN, SOIL, WATER, FOOD

Plant in full sun in a well drained soil. A slightly alkaline or neutral soil (with a pH of 6.5–7) will give the best results. Keep plants

moist but do not over-water during dry periods. Excessive water will produce leaves at the expense of roots.

FLOWERS

Once plants have flowered they set copious amounts of seed. By this time, however, the roots will have become tough and almost unusable. The 'seed' is actually a cluster of seeds held together in a cork-like case.

GROWING FROM CUTTINGS OR SEED

Sow seeds directly where you want them to grow, as seedlings transplant badly. Soak the seeds in water overnight before sowing. Look for non-bolting varieties that suit your season and climate. Round, oval, long and tapering types are available.

CARE / MAINTENANCE

Thinned seedlings will grow if they are treated to generous quantities of liquid fertiliser once replanted.

PLANTING

Plant seedlings with care and keep moist until they are growing strongly. Beetroot is sensitive to soil acidity so it pays to add a little lime to most New Zealand soils before planting. Don't add too much, however, or you will have very weak, anaemic-looking plants. Soil that has been well manured for a previous leaf crop such as cabbages is perfect. Beetroot is a good inter-cropping plant that will also grow well in the filtered shade of taller plants.

HARVESTING

Start harvesting 9-10 weeks after sowing. Small roots are more tender and tastier than large ones. The roots with the leafy tops removed will keep for several weeks in a cupboard or for several months in the crisper bin of the refrigerator.

PESTS AND DISEASES

Leaf miner, leaf spot, mildew, rust and nutrient deficiency can sometimes affect beetroot. Fungal and insect pests are best treated with a suitable spray. Be aware that nutrient deficiency is often the result of over-liming.

IN POTS AND TUBS

Beetroot are easy to grow in pots and tubs. The foliage is attractive and some types are quite colourful. Beets are not hungry consumers of water and will thrive in containers with the minimum of care.

Bok Choy
(Brassica Rapa)

GROWING TIMES

Late summer and early autumn sowings or plantings will result in plants that don't bolt to seed. They will grow slowly through the winter, maturing in the spring and early summer. Seeds sown in spring and summer often bolt to seed. Plants are usually ready for harvest 8–10 weeks after sowing.

HEIGHT / SPREAD

20 cm x 20 cm.

FROST HARDINESS

Moderately frost hardy.

SUN, SOIL, WATER, FOOD

Plant in a fertile soil that has been packed with plenty of compost and general purpose fertiliser. Keep plants well watered and feed with a liquid fertiliser at least once a fortnight.

FLOWERS

Plants flower freely and produce considerable quantities of seed. Allow a few plants to flower so that you can save the seed and sow another crop.

GROWING FROM CUTTINGS OR SEED

Sow seed directly into the garden in clumps and then thin out all but the strongest plant in each clump. Seedlings don't transplant well and often bolt to seed, especially when the weather is hot and dry. Sow seed every 3–4 weeks. This keeps a succession of plants available. Bok choy is tolerant of both heat and cold, and will grow throughout the year in many parts of the country. The young seedlings should be set out in full sun 30–40 cm apart in a well prepared, fertile soil. Keep well watered in the late summer and autumn. Some varieties do well in hot, moist weather and can be ready for use as soon as 5 weeks, while others grow best in cool climates and mature more slowly.

CARE / MAINTENANCE

Sow seed often and keep the plants growing quickly. This will produce the most tender and tastiest leaves.

PLANTING

Dig the bed deeply and incorporate plenty of well-rotted compost. Add a dressing of general purpose fertiliser several weeks before planting. Liquid fertiliser will also help produce tender and tasty plants.

HARVESTING

Pick when the plants are young and tender and use quickly. This crop deteriorates rapidly. It will seldom last more than a few days in the fridge.

PESTS AND DISEASES

The same problems that affect other members of the brassica family also affect bok choy. Aphids will attack, as will white butterfly caterpillars. Spray with a suitable insecticide.

IN POTS AND TUBS

Although the decorative rosettes of bok choy and other members of the Chinensis group of brassicas are attractive in pots and containers, they mature quickly and need replacing often, and are for that reason probably best left in the garden.

Broccoli

(Brassica Oleracea, Cymosa Group Cultivar)

GROWING TIMES

Sow seeds in the spring and plant out in the early summer when the soil has warmed. Plants will continue to grow through the winter. Heading broccoli such as the 'Romanesco' type do better in cold areas, while the more usual sprouting broccoli will grow successfully throughout a mild northern winter.

HEIGHT / SPREAD
1 m x 50 cm.

FROST HARDINESS
Moderately frost hardy. Broccoli does best in areas with cool winters but can be grown in most climate zones.

SUN, SOIL, WATER, FOOD
When the plants are developing give them plenty of nitrogenous fertiliser or apply a liquid fertiliser every two or three weeks. Prepare the ground well before planting broccoli. Plenty of compost, a little lime and a dressing of general purpose fertiliser will produce the best heads.

FLOWERS
The flower heads are the edible parts and must be eaten before the flowers begin to open. The 'Romanesco' hybrids are more like cauliflowers in appearance and flavour. The tight hemispherical heads form many neat conical points. They are usually pale green in colour.

GROWING FROM CUTTINGS OR SEED
Sow seeds in a seed bed in spring and plant out in summer in rows 60 cm apart. They can then be left to develop over winter and picked over a long season from spring until summer. Once broccoli flower they stop growing.

CARE / MAINTENANCE
Prick out seedlings when they have formed their first true leaf. Grow them in individual pots until they are 10–15 cm tall. Seeds can also be sown directly into the soil in clumps the same distance apart. Once the clumps germinate and grow they can be thinned out, leaving only the most vigorous seedlings.

PLANTING
Plant in a lime rich, moist, well drained soil in full sun. Seedlings can be raised in seed trays and planted out 6–8 weeks later. Plant in a sheltered, sunny spot in a soil that has previously been used for a different crop. Shop bought seedlings should be treated similarly. Make successive sowings over a period of weeks for a continuing supply. Nine plants at each sowing should be enough for the average family.

HARVESTING
Cut the main head of the plant when it is still tight. All types of broccoli are best picked and eaten when the heads are young and tight before the yellow flowers open. Once the buds begin to open the taste deteriorates quickly. Remove with a slanting cut so that water does not collect in the cut and cause the plant to rot. Use broccoli as quickly as possible after it is harvested. Heading broccoli should be pulled out once the florets are cut. Sprouting broccoli, on the other hand, will continue to produce long after the central heads have been harvested.

PESTS AND DISEASES
Aphids will often attack broccoli. Spray with a suitable insecticide. Black leg is another problem that attacks many members of the brassica family. Stems go black causing the entire plant to collapse. It is difficult to control but scraping away the soil from the stem and treating it with a fungicide is sometimes effective. If plants become infected do not plant any members of the brassica family in the same area for at least two seasons. Caterpillars of the white butterfly will devastate a broccoli crop. Control by spraying, sprinkling with derris dust or removing the pests by hand.

IN POTS AND TUBS
The 'Romanesco' broccolis are highly decorative plants. In a rich soil that is well drained and kept moist they will produce well, while at the same time providing colour and interest in the winter and spring garden.

Cabbage

(Brassica Oleracea)

GROWING TIMES

Cabbage and most of its relatives are cool season vegetables. They grow best if they are harvested when the temperatures are below 20°C. Sow seed in late spring. Excellent red cultivars include 'Greengold', a late maturing cabbage, and 'Mammoth Red Rock'. 'Hawke' is green but very hardy and long lasting.

HEIGHT / SPREAD

Depends on type. Small heading types are available as are larger growing varieties. Space small varieties 30–50 cm apart but allow 60–75 cm between larger varieties.

FROST HARDINESS

Some types are very frost hardy. Choose a type that suits your season and climate.

SUN, SOIL, WATER, FOOD

Cabbages like full sun, good drainage and a rich, well composted soil. Use a general purpose fertiliser at 60–120 g per square metre. A pH of 6.5–7.5 is best. Feed cabbages at planting time and again in 4 weeks.

FLOWERS

Flowers are yellow and attractive. Seed sets easily.

GROWING FROM CUTTINGS OR SEED

Plants are raised easily from seed. 9–12 plants from a single sowing are more than adequate for the average family.

CARE / MAINTENANCE

After cutting cabbages leave the trunks and they will sprout, forming useful yet tiny cabbages and leaves.

PLANTING

Cabbages can be grown at almost any time of the year. Add a little lime to the soil several weeks before planting to help prevent club root disease (this disease often afflicts members of the cabbage family). Ten days after adding the lime dig in a little general fertiliser that is low in nitrogen, leave for a few days and then plant out your seedlings. This will ensure that the plants don't produce soft growth that can be damaged by winter frosts.

HARVESTING

Harvest either as the young heads are forming or later when they are fully mature. Cabbages can be left in the garden during the colder months.

PESTS AND DISEASES

Black leg is a fungal disease that will cause the stem to blacken and rot. At the first signs of this disease scratch the soil away from the stem and apply a suitable fungicide. If the infection is severe avoid growing any members of the brassica family in the area for at least two years. White butterfly caterpillars can be controlled by using derris dust, or other non-chemical insecticides.

IN POTS AND TUBS

Smaller growing types such as 'Mini' will form heads 10 cm across. They make ideal container plants. 'Purple Head', 'Hardora' and 'Mammoth Red Rock' are large-heading types with attractively coloured foliage.

Capsicum
(Capsicum Annuum)

GROWING TIMES

Capsicum are warm season vegetables and grow best in tropical and sub tropical areas. They are slow to develop where the spring and early summer is cool, and need to be sown under glass in August for planting out as soon as the weather is warm.

HEIGHT / SPREAD

Up to 1.8 m x 40–50 cm.

FROST HARDINESS

Frost tender. In warm areas they can be treated as biennials, but in cool areas they will need to be replanted each spring and early summer.

SUN, SOIL, WATER, FOOD

Capsicum need to be planted in full sun and in a position protected from cold winds. They will grow in light or heavy soils, as long as they have plenty of warmth and moisture in the growing period. Compost or animal manure added to the soil several weeks before planting will encourage healthy plants and increase crop yield. When fruit is setting, water with a liquid fertiliser, or side dress the plants with a monthly application of a small amount of fertiliser or well decayed animal manure or compost.

FLOWERS

Flowers are not especially attractive to bees. To increase pollination plant bee-attracting herbs such as lavender, thyme or borage in the vicinity, or pollinate by hand with a soft watercolour brush.

GROWING FROM CUTTINGS OR SEED

Seeds are slow to germinate. The process can be sped up a little by soaking them overnight in warm water before sowing. Seedlings are often readily available from garden centres. Buy stocky vigorous plants with deep green leaves for best results.

CARE / MAINTENANCE

Allow the large bell shaped varieties to set 5-8 fruit. Pick off any other flowers. If plants are subject to wind they may need staking.

PLANTING

Prepare the soil well before planting. Add large quantities of compost or animal manure, or enrich the soil with a generous dressing of general purpose fertiliser with a N P K of 10 / 4 / 6. Plant 60 cm apart in a well drained, sunny position.

HARVESTING

Always pick capsicum as soon as they are ripe. This enables the plant to spend its energy on setting more fruit. Cut rather than pull fruit from the plant, so that the brittle stems are not broken and the bearing potential of the plant lessened.

PESTS AND DISEASES

Aphids and shield bugs will sometimes attack capsicum. Spray with an insecticide or remove pests with a sharp jet of water from the hose.

IN POTS AND TUBS

Capsicum make very decorative pot plants. They will grow well in pots set in the sun, as long as they are kept regularly watered. Chilli peppers, also members of the capsicum family, make very decorative container plants.

GROWING FROM CUTTINGS OR SEED

Sow seeds directly where you want carrots to grow as they are difficult to transplant. Prepare the soil well so that it is fine and crumbly. Sow seeds thinly in a shallow drill 1 cm deep and cover with light compost or a sandy soil mixture. Space drills 30 cm apart. Carrots mature in 10–12 weeks.

CARE / MAINTENANCE

When they are large enough to be used for salads you should thin the young plants to 5–7 cm apart. This enables the remaining carrots to develop fully.

PLANTING

4–6 m at each sowing will produce a continuous supply for a family of five. Make sowings every five weeks through the season.

Carrot

(Daucus Carota)

GROWING TIMES

Easy to grow from seed at any time from spring until autumn.

HEIGHT / SPREAD

Height up to 25 cm. Varieties with long tapering roots and cylindrical roots suit light deep soils. Stumpy and small root varieties suit heavy soils.

FROST HARDINESS

Carrots are susceptible to frost and should not be sown until spring unless you have a sunny, frost free position.

SUN, SOIL, WATER, FOOD

Sow carrots in well-worked, well-drained ground that has been heavily manured for a previous crop. Carrots resent fresh manure or fertiliser. Add a little lime to the soil before sowing.

FLOWERS

Insignificant.

HARVESTING

Start culling the crop when the carrots reach less than finger size. Young carrots are sweet and tender. Over mature carrots often become woody and tasteless.

PESTS AND DISEASES

Aphids, leaf spot and deformed roots will often affect carrots. Aphids can be treated with soapy water or a suitable insecticide, while leaf spot needs to be treated with a fungicide. Distorted roots often occur when the crop is grown in a heavy soil or when thinning is delayed for too long.

IN POTS AND TUBS

Stump rooted varieties are especially suited for pot culture.

Celery

(Apium Graveolens Var Dulce)

GROWING TIMES

Start seedlings indoors in August and plant out in mid spring. Celery is a cool weather crop that can be sown or planted from August until March.

HEIGHT / SPREAD

Varies depending on type. Small types grow up to 23 cm, while large varieties can reach 60 cm. Spread is 50 cm.

FROST HARDINESS

Celery is susceptible to both spring and winter frost, so make sure you plant them out after the last frost in your area. Be prepared to cover your crop in the late autumn to protect them from frost just prior to the maturing of the plant. Although severe frost will damage the plant, the inner leaves should still be good.

SUN, SOIL, WATER, FOOD

Full sun or part shade is suitable. Celery should be grown quickly in a warm, well drained part of the garden. Enrich the soil with plenty of compost and/or well rotted animal manure. The pH of the soil should be about 6.5–7.5. Add a little lime to most New Zealand soils and keep plants well watered during dry spells.

FLOWERS

Harvest flowers when still young and tender. Don't allow plants to go to seed as the quality of the stalks will be ruined.

GROWING FROM CUTTINGS OR SEED

The seeds are tiny and difficult to sow and thin. Sow seeds in individual pots or containers, putting as few as possible in each pot. The seeds may take 14–20 days to germinate. After they have germinated and are large enough to thin, remove all but two or three. As they continue to grow, thin to one per pot. Transplant outdoors after all danger of frost has passed. Space plants 30–40 cm each way.

CARE / MAINTENANCE

To blanch celery wrap several sheets of newspaper around each plant to a height of about 40 cm and tie loosely with string. Do this at least three weeks before harvesting. Blanched celery is usually sweeter and more tender than unblanched. Varieties that require blanching are now little used in the home garden as they require a lot of extra work.

PLANTING

Ordinary celery requires a long growing season of up to 150 days. Add general purpose fertiliser and/or compost as you work the soil before planting, and side dress regularly throughout the growing season. Without proper care and conditions, the stalks can become very dry, tough and stringy. There are a limited number of varieties of celery on the market. 'Tall Utah' is a popular, strong growing strain with deep green leaves and sweet, tender stems. It matures in about four months and does not need blanching.

HARVESTING

Harvest celery by cutting the whole plant at ground level, or pick the outside stems as you need them.

PESTS AND DISEASES

Leaf spot, slugs and blight are the most common problems that beset celery. Blight occurs most frequently in wet weather. Stalks may split as a result of dry weather. Both problems should be treated early with a suitable fungicide.

IN POTS AND TUBS

Celery can be easily grown in pots and tubs as long as water requirements are attended to.

Chicory & Endive

(Chicorium Intybus & Chicorium Endivia)

GROWING TIMES

Perennial types will grow all year round, even where the winters are cold.

HEIGHT / SPREAD

Will grow up to 60 x 60 cm or more, depending on the variety. Low growing types seldom reach more than 30 cm high and wide.

FROST HARDINESS

Mostly frost hardy.

SUN, SOIL, WATER, FOOD

Sow or plant during late summer in full sun in a fine, humus-rich soil that is moist and well drained. Apply a liquid fertiliser every second week to boost growth.

FLOWERS

Clear blue flowers are produced throughout the late spring and summer. They can be added to salads as a garnish or simply enjoyed in the garden. Both chicorium intybus and chicorium endivia set seed easily and germinate rapidly.

GROWING FROM CUTTINGS OR SEED

Sow the seeds in clumps 1 cm deep in rows 30 cm apart. Thin the seedlings, leaving the strongest ones spaced at 5–7 cm.

CARE / MAINTENANCE

Both chicorium intybus and chicorium endivia are best eaten when the leaves or tender 'chicons' (shoots) are young. 'Witloof' is a popular forcing type.

PLANTING

Plant at least 15–20 plants in a well drained soil if you want to harvest chicorium intybus chicons. Six or seven chicorium endivia plants will be adequate for the average family.

HARVESTING

Chicorium endivia is grown mainly for its

of the root so that it is about 20 cm long. Place four or five roots in a pot of sandy soil, filling it so that only the crowns are visible. Fill another pot of the same size with peat moss and invert it over the roots so that all light is excluded. The new shoots should be harvested when they are 15–20 cm tall. If the pots are placed in a warm position this will take about four weeks.

PESTS AND DISEASES
Almost trouble free. Use bait to protect plants from slugs and snails.

IN POTS AND TUBS
All types of chicory are easy to grow in pots and containers. Coloured forms such as 'Palla Rosa', 'Red Verona' and 'Castelfranco' are attractive and useful garden plants.

Cucumber
(Cucumis Sativus)

GROWING TIMES
Late spring and summer when the soil is warm and moist. Plants usually bear 8–12 weeks after sowing.

HEIGHT / SPREAD
They will grow up to 45 cm and spread over a 1.8 m area if left to their own devices. In small gardens they can be trained on a trellis or up strings tacked to a fence to save space.

FROST HARDINESS
Not at all.

SUN, SOIL, WATER, FOOD
Plant in full sun or part shade in a warm, fertile, crumbly soil, in a sheltered position. Natives of India, it is hardly surprising that these plants need heat as well as moisture to flourish. In cool areas they are best grown in greenhouses. Dry air and a moist soil are preferable as humid conditions can encourage fungal disease. When flowering begins side dress plants with a highly nitrogenous fertiliser (NPK 10 / 4 / 6), avoiding

leaves, which resemble lettuce but have a sharper flavour. Chicorium intybus (chicory, witloof, raddicchio) is grown mainly for its edible roots and tasty, slightly bitter leaves. Blanched shoots (chicons) make a delicious addition to winter and spring salads. To raise chicons, harvest (dig) the roots in late autumn, about 16 weeks after sowing. Cut the leaves off about 5 cm above the top, taking care not to damage the growing point. Shorten the bottom contact with the foliage. Liquid fertilisers are also available commercially. Apply every six weeks.

FLOWERS

Small yellow, funnel shaped flowers occur in clusters of two or three between the leaf stalk and the stem. Hand pollinate them with a soft watercolour brush if you want a good crop of cucumbers.

GROWING FROM CUTTINGS OR SEED

Dust seeds with a fungicide or powdered sulphur before planting. This helps to control damping off disease, to which cucumber seedlings are prone. Sow more seeds than you need as germination is often patchy. Thin out,

leaving only the strongest plants. Cucumbers can also be sown indoors in small pots in September so that they are ready to plant out as soon as the warm weather arrives.

CARE / MAINTENANCE

When plants are growing strongly and have made six or seven leaves pinch out the growing tips to encourage lateral shoots. If side shoots are 60 cm long and show no sign of bearing, pinch out the tips. After the first set of fruit pinch out the side shoots.

PLANTING

Four to six plants are usually adequate for the average family.

HARVESTING

Pick as soon as the cucumbers are 15–20 cm long, to encourage further fruit production. Apple cucumbers should be picked when they are tennis ball size.

PESTS AND DISEASES

Cucumbers are susceptible to mildew although the long green types have a tougher skin and are more resistant. Plant them in spring or early summer for a summer and autumn harvest. Red spider mite, white fly, downy mildew and powdery mildew all affect cucumbers. Treat fungal diseases with a suitable spray or dust with flowers of sulphur. White fly and spider mite can be controlled with an insecticide/miticide or, if growing indoors, with bright yellow sticky boards. Remove weeds that can act as a host to whitefly.

IN POTS AND TUBS

Cucumbers prefer to climb. They bear better and remain healthy if the fruit is kept away from the soil. A simple trellis or tee-pee structure can be placed in a container and the vine trained and tied. Cucumbers are very decorative plants.

Garlic

(Allium Sativum)

GROWING TIMES
From mid winter to mid summer (6 months to harvest).

HEIGHT / SPREAD
Plants produce 45–70 cm flowering stalks in summer, and grow to 30 cm wide.

FROST HARDINESS
Frost hardy.

SOIL, SUN, WATER, FOOD
Grows easily in well-drained garden soil – add lime and general garden fertiliser or blood and bone. Full sun or part shade is best.

FLOWERS
Flowers before mid summer. When the flower heads fall over dig up, plait and store in a warm, dry, airy place out of the sun.

GROWING FROM CUTTINGS OR SEED
Divide bulb and plant the cloves in mid winter. Garlic can be grown from seed but this is a slow process. The clove method is quicker.

CARE / MAINTENANCE
Spent flower heads can be cut off just before harvesting.

PLANTING
Remove the outside husk and break each bulb into individual cloves without baring the flesh. The soil should not be heavy or sodden but friable and moist. Plant the cloves 10-12 cm apart, with the pointed end up. Fertilise the soil several weeks before planting. Place in a 6 cm furrow and cover lightly with soil. A few side dressings of fertiliser during the growing season will boost the size of the final crop. The soil around them should always be kept moist, not wet.

HARVESTING
Harvest when the tops fall over and die. Leave them to dry in a warm airy place for several days, then plait the tops together or place them in old net onion bags. A good circulation of air is essential to prevent bulbs from rotting. 24 weeks is the more usual maturing time, although under ideal conditions cloves may mature in just 16 weeks.

PESTS AND DISEASES

Aphids will sometimes attack garlic. Wash them off with the hose or use simple soap sprays. Neck rot can attack newly harvested bulbs. Storing them in a warm place with good ventilation will help prevent this disease.

IN POTS AND TUBS

Garlic will grow quite happily in a sunny window box or pot as long as the soil doesn't dry out.

Leek

(Allium Porrum)

GROWING TIMES

Leeks can be grown at almost any time of the year but the best crops will be produced from spring and summer sown plants. It is important that they get plenty of moisture during the growing period if the stalks are to be sweet and tender. The mature plants are most useful during the winter months. Leeks take on average 150 days to reach maturity from seed, or 110 days from seedlings.

HEIGHT / SPREAD

Varies. The very fat stemmed 'Mammoth Blanche' spreads up to 6 cm in diameter, while the stem grows up to 1 metre or more in height.

FROST HARDINESS

Leeks are amongst the hardiest of vegetables. Established during the warmer months, they can be left in the ground during autumn and winter and lifted as required, without spoiling.

SUN, SOIL, WATER, FOOD

Leeks prefer a sunny position and well drained soil that has been deeply dug. Add plenty of compost to the soil when planting, as well as a little general purpose fertiliser. The addition of lime will produce better crops, especially on acid soils.

FLOWERS

Summer flowering in the main.

GROWING FROM CUTTINGS OR SEED

Plants that are left to flower are of little culinary use but will provide good crops of seed that can be saved and sown again.

CARE / MAINTENANCE

When planting seedlings trim the roots and leaves by one half their length.

PLANTING

Drop into dibble holes or into a trench 8–10 cm deep. Space seedlings at 15–20 cm intervals. Make sure that the holes are deeper than the white portion of the seedling. Once the seedlings are in place water them and leave. Don't bother to cover with soil. They will firm themselves as they grow. Keep well watered in dry weather.

HARVESTING

Dig up each leek with a trowel rather than pulling it from the ground. Pulling them up will usually result in parts of the plant breaking away or snapping, leaving most of the stalk in the ground. Side shoots with roots attached are sometimes formed. These can be detached and returned to the garden where they will grow into mature plants.

PESTS AND DISEASES

Downy mildew, rust and white rot will sometimes attack. These fungal diseases can be treated with chemical or natural sprays. Thrips can also affect leek crops. Spray with an insecticide or wash these pests off with the hose. Natural insecticide sprays are also effective in limiting the spread of thrips.

IN POTS AND TUBS

Leeks will grow just as readily in pots and tubs as they do in the garden. All they require is a rich, well drained soil and plenty of moisture during the growing period.

Lettuce

(Lactuca Sativa)

GROWING TIMES

Many lettuce will grow happily through a mild winter. In the main they resent frosty weather, flourishing in temperatures which range from 10–16°C.

HEIGHT / SPREAD

Upright 'Mini Coss' grow 20 cm high x 6 cm across. Others vary greatly in height and spread depending on the variety. Small varieties can be spaced 20 cm apart, larger types 30 cm.

FROST HARDINESS

'Merveille des Quatre Saisons' is, as the name implies, a 'four seasons' lettuce. It can be sown almost all year round and tolerates some cold weather. The compact, neatly formed head is not only a splendid salad lettuce but is also good to look at. The leaves are a soft lime green, frosted with a pale tint of red-magenta.

SUN, SOIL, WATER, FOOD

Prepare the soil well by adding plenty of well rotted manure or compost. The soil should also be well drained. A pre-planting fertiliser with a NPK of 5 / 7 / 4 should also be scattered at a rate of 100 g per square metre. Seedlings are best raised in boxes and transplanted out when they are 5–6 cm high. Water plants regularly in the summer. Every day would not be too much in hot weather. Using a liquid fertiliser will also ensure quick growth and sweet succulent plants.

FLOWERS

In mid to late summer as temperatures rise and the soil dries many lettuce plants will race to seed. Flowers are insignificant but plants will set considerable quantities of seed that can be collected, stored and then sown again.

GROWING FROM CUTTINGS OR SEED

Sow seeds 5 cm deep in a fine seed mix and water sparingly. Once they have germinated and developed, you can sow in spring, summer and autumn to ensure a succession of lettuce for the table.

CARE / MAINTENANCE

Thin seedlings to 20–30 cm. Leaf lettuces (lactuca sativa crispa) are useful in that they do not form a head and therefore do not need to be picked completely at any one time. Rather they can be progressively plucked and enjoyed a leaf or two at a time.

PLANTING

Twelve maturing plants are more than adequate for a medium sized family. Sow seeds every 3–4 weeks to keep a succession of plants available for the table.

HARVESTING

Lettuce is often ready to use in 8–10 weeks, depending on the variety. Each sowing will usually provide at least four weeks' harvesting. Cut or pull plants in the morning when they are fresh and crisp. They store well in the refrigerator.

PESTS AND DISEASES

Slugs and snails, aphids, downy mildew, poor seed germination and bolting are all problems that can affect lettuce. Inspect plants regularly to remove slugs and snails or use a bait. Aphids can be treated with soapy water or an insecticide. Downy mildew is best treated with a suitable fungicide at the first sign of the disease. Once established it is difficult to cure. Seeds will germinate better if the soil is well drained, warm and moist. Bolting (premature flowering) is usually the result of choosing the wrong variety for the season.

IN POTS AND TUBS

Lettuce, especially the red, frilled and oak leaf varieties, are not only easy to grow in pots and containers but are also very decorative. Try 'Red Sails', 'Lollo Rosso', 'New Red Fire' or 'Rouge d'Hiver' depending on the season.

Mustard – Giant Red

(Brassica Rapa)

GROWING TIMES

This useful mustard produces in winter and spring, and is very frost hardy and slow to bolt. Sow seeds in late summer and plant seedlings out in late autumn and early winter.

HEIGHT / SPREAD

30 x 35 cm.

FROST HARDINESS

Very frost hardy.

SUN, SOIL, WATER, FOOD

Plant in full sun in a rich, well drained soil. Compost will produce large leaves but generally this is a very undemanding crop to grow.

FLOWERS

Attractive yellow flowers are produced in the summer. Large quantities of seed often result in a plethora of self sown plants.

GROWING FROM CUTTINGS OR SEED

Seeds germinate easily and seedlings are easily transplanted.

CARE / MAINTENANCE

Space at least 30 cm apart. Pick the leaves regularly. Cut the flower heads as soon as they form to prevent the plant from bolting to seed as the weather warms.

PLANTING

Plant in a rich soil and rotate all members of the cabbage family with other vegetables each year.

HARVESTING

The colourful green and maroon leaves can be harvested young and used in salads, or pickled or boiled when they are more mature. They can also be stuffed and steamed or baked. The large savoy leaf is tender and finely flavoured, with a gentle mustard taste.

PESTS AND DISEASES

Generally disease free. Aphids may attack in warm weather. Spray with soapy water or wash them off with the hose. Otherwise use an insecticide.

IN POTS AND TUBS

The giant red mustard grows well and looks very attractive in pots.

Peas
(Pisum Sativum)

GROWING TIMES

Peas are a cool season crop. They can be sown from autumn to spring in mild areas. In areas where the winters are cold and frosty plant in mid-winter to late spring.

HEIGHT / SPREAD

Some varieties will grow over 2 m high and as much as 50 cm wide. The snow pea 'Snow Queen' is a mangetout type where the pod is eaten whole. It also grows to almost 2 m and needs to be supported.

FROST HARDINESS

Moderately frost hardy.

SUN, SOIL, WATER, FOOD

Plant in full sun in a moist, fertile, well drained soil. Choose a part of the garden that is sheltered from strong winds. A little lime, dolomite and superphosphate added to the soil in the previous autumn will ensure good results. Keep weeds down and water generously when the weather is dry.

FLOWERS

Flowers are usually white. Some varieties produce red flowers.

GROWING FROM CUTTINGS OR SEED

Plant a generous amount of seed at monthly intervals for a succession. Pick pods regularly to encourage growth. Sow seeds in a soil that

PLANTING

Sow at least a 3–5 m row for adequate cropping. Sow again at four weekly intervals to keep a succession of peas for the table.

HARVESTING

The mangetout or sugar snap peas need to be eaten when they are still young and the pods flat. The tendrils, like the pods, can also be used as garnish, added to stir fries, steamed, or eaten raw. All other types also need to be picked fresh and eaten while they are still young and tender.

PESTS AND DISEASES

Birds will sometimes attack the pea crop. Covering with fine wire-netting will prevent a lot of damage, especially when the plants are young. Root rot can be avoided by planting in a free-draining soil and using a fungicide at planting time. Slugs and snails will also devastate a pea crop. Lay a bait or remove by hand and clear away any rotting foliage that might be harbouring these destructive pests. Also watch for mildew, blight and mites, and act at the first signs of disease.

IN POTS AND TUBS

Dwarf peas can be grown in pots, but in order to get a reasonable crop they are best grown in the garden. They are not particularly attractive container plants.

has been well prepared. Break up the soil to a fine tilth and add a generous dressing of a fertiliser with a N P K of 5 / 7 / 4 either side of the seed furrow. This enables the growing plants to access the food as they need it. Plant seeds 5 cm apart. Cover the seed with a 4 cm layer of soil and firm them into place with the flat side of a rake. Allow at least 2 m between rows of tall varieties and 20–40 cm between rows for dwarf varieties.

CARE / MAINTENANCE

Train through several suspended layers of wide wire-netting or between stakes interlaced with strong string. Peas can also be planted up bamboo towers, trellis and fences. Start them climbing by training up twiggy pieces of manuka brush.

Potato

(Solanum Tuberosum)

GROWING TIMES

Varieties are divided into early, early main and main crop. It pays to choose varieties that suit not only your soil but also the season. 'Cliff's Kidney' is an early crop potato best planted in early spring, 'Arran Banner' an early main, and 'Rua' a main crop potato best planted in late spring or early summer.

HEIGHT / SPREAD
80–90 cm x 50 cm depending on variety.

FROST HARDINESS
Not frost hardy.

SUN, SOIL, WATER, FOOD
Potatoes of all types grow best in peaty, acid soils in a sunny, well-drained position. They also grow well in sandy soil if plenty of well decayed compost and manure has been mixed in before planting. Blood and bone or a balanced fertiliser also helps get good results.

FLOWERS
Flowers are attractive, occurring in pendant clusters of white, pale violet and soft purple.

GROWING FROM CUTTINGS OR SEED
Potatoes can be grown from seed. The usual way, however, is to grow them from small seed potatoes or tubers. Tubers suitable for planting should be 50–60 g in weight and well sprouted. Plant seed potatoes 5 cm deep and 25–30 cm apart, in rows 50–60 cm apart. This makes the process of 'earthing up' easier (see below).

CARE / MAINTENANCE
When the leaves are 20 cm high build up the soil ('earth up') around the plants, covering some of the new shoots and lower leaves. Continue the process at two weekly intervals until the plants flower and begin to die back. This process protects plants from late frost, warms the soil and helps retain moisture. It also prevents the tubers from greening when they are exposed to light, thereby ensuring a better crop.

PLANTING
For light soils the experts recommend 'Arran Banner' or 'Glen Ilam'. Types such as 'Arran Chief' grow better in heavy soils. The 'Peru Peru' likes a light soil and plenty of compost and will grow in cold weather. 'Ilam Hardy' and 'Red King Edward' grow best in the cooler south, whereas varieties such as 'Tahi' and 'Rua' flourish in the north.

HARVESTING
Harvest after 16–20 weeks. This will be about four weeks after the plants have finished flowering. Dig only those plants that you require. In loose soils it is even possible to scratch out the few that you need, leaving the rest of the plant to continue growing. Potatoes for storage should only be dug when the stalks and foliage have dried and died off completely.

PESTS AND DISEASES
Blight, aphids, thrips and viral diseases can attack potatoes. Treat with suitable insecticides or fungicides. Always ensure that you plant only virus-free tubers. Tubers that are well drained, well fed and in an open position seldom succumb to disease.

IN POTS AND TUBS

Potatoes can be successfully grown in pots and tubs. Fill a large bucket with 10–15 cm of soil and mix in a generous handful of a fertiliser containing a NPK of 5 / 7 / 4. Place a seed potato on top of this mix and cover it with soil. As the potato sprouts cover it every second week until the bucket is full. Allow the plant to mature, flower and die back. Simply tip out the bucket and secure the crop.

Pumpkin – winter variety

(Curcubita Maxima)

GROWING TIMES

Pumpkins require a long, warm growing season of at least 14 weeks. Plant them in late spring, summer and autumn depending on local conditions. All curcubits are quick growing and the winter pumpkin is no exception.

HEIGHT / SPREAD

Many varieties are available, with some spreading over a wide area. Others (such as 'Golden Nugget' and 'Crown Prince') are compact bush varieties with small, late maturing fruit.

FROST HARDINESS

Frost tender.

SUN, SOIL, WATER, FOOD

Full sun and moist but well drained conditions are essential for good germination. Prepare the soil by adding plenty of well decayed compost and animal manure. Dust the soil with pre-planting fertiliser with a NPK of 5 / 7 / 4. Water regularly when fruit begins to set.

FLOWERS

Large, decorative, bell shaped, orange/yellow flowers are produced from summer until early autumn.

GROWING FROM CUTTINGS OR SEED

Sow seeds as soon as the soil is warm. Early sowings can be made in pots and the plants transferred later into the garden. Do not over water or the seeds will rot. Seedlings emerge quickly in 5–10 days.

CARE / MAINTENANCE

Pumpkins can be trained up over walls and arches or left to trail along the ground. Cultivate the soil between clumps until the vines cover the soil. Pinch out the main stems to promote lateral growth and a heavier set of fruit. Lift growing fruit above the ground with a piece of board, brick or stone to ensure that the skin is always dry.

PLANTING

Six plants should be more than enough for the average family. Winter pumpkins bear heavily and some such as 'Triamble' and 'Queensland Blue' store well and can last through the winter.

HARVESTING

Harvest pumpkins as the vines shrivel and die and the fruit is fully mature. Mature fruit tastes better and stores well, whereas immature fruit can be insipid and rots quickly. When pumpkins are mature they snap easily from the vine. The stalk should not be removed.

PESTS AND DISEASES

Fungal diseases are often a problem when it comes to growing pumpkins. Dust seeds with a fungicide before planting and ensure that the soil is rich in organic matter and always moist but never wet. Mulch plants in the summer with sawdust or grass clippings to ensure a cool, moist root run.

IN POTS AND TUBS

Pumpkins are highly decorative plants with attractive heart shaped leaves, colourful flowers and spectacular fruit. Even the larger growing varieties can be contained in pots and trained over arches, walls and fences.

Silver Beet

(Beta Vulgaris)

GROWING TIMES

In many parts of New Zealand it is possible to have silver beet growing almost all year round. Sow seeds from early spring and autumn for harvesting in 55-65 days. Silver beet planted in the hot summer months will bolt to seed, producing a poor crop of leaves. 'Ruby chard', the red silver beet, is said to withstand heat better than the green type.

HEIGHT / SPREAD

Up to 70 cm x 40 cm.

FROST HARDINESS

Moderately frost hardy.

SUN, SOIL, WATER, FOOD

Dig plenty of well rotted compost into the soil, then scatter a pre-planting fertiliser with a NPK of 5 / 7 / 4 and rake it in. Sow seeds in punnets or straight into the soil where you want them to grow. Sow three or four seeds 1 cm deep in clumps 40 cm apart. Water gently. When the seedlings appear, thin out to the strongest seedling.

FLOWERS

Flowers are insignificant but produce large volumes of valuable seed.

GROWING FROM CUTTINGS OR SEED

Plants are easily grown from seed. Before sowing soak the seeds for several hours and dust with a fungicide or flowers of sulphur.

CARE / MAINTENANCE

Pick regularly to encourage fresh growth and remove any stems that attempt to flower (unless you want the seeds). Once plants go to seed they cease to produce useable leaves.

PLANTING

You can sow seeds and plant seedlings at almost any time of the year in a rich, well drained soil. Mulching plants will help conserve moisture and keep them going in the hottest months of the year. For large green leaves grow 'Fordhook Giant'. If you want colour in the garden try 'Rainbow Chard', as this variety produces leaves with red, purple, yellow or pink stems.

HARVESTING

Pick leaves when they are large enough to use. Pick by breaking the leaves away from the stem with a downward motion, much as you would when picking rhubarb. Never pick all the leaves on a single plant. Leave at least five leaves to help the plant regenerate.

PESTS AND DISEASES

Leaf miners, leaf spot and mildew will sometimes attack silver beet. Use suitable fungicide or insecticide sprays. Help avoid disease by feeding generously and watering well in hot weather. Give side dressings of liquid fertiliser every 10–14 days.

IN POTS AND TUBS

Silver beet is highly decorative and easy to grow in tubs and planters.

Spinach

(Spinacia Oleracea)

GROWING TIMES

Two kinds are traditionally grown: the marginally frost hardy summer spinach and the fully frost hardy prickly-seeded winter type.

HEIGHT / SPREAD

Forms a rosette of leaves 20–30 cm across x 40 cm high. A flower stalk from 60 cm to 1 m high is produced as the plant sets seed.

FROST HARDINESS

Depends on type.

SUN, SOIL, WATER, FOOD

Plant in full sun in a moist, well drained soil and mulch in the summer to conserve moisture. Spinach grows best in a deeply dug soil that has been enriched with plenty of compost and a light dressing of a fertiliser containing a NPK of 5 / 7 / 4.

FLOWERS

Insignificant green flowers that readily set seed.

GROWING FROM CUTTINGS OR SEED

Sow seeds in spring or autumn, thinning seedlings so that plants are 25 cm apart. Harvest the first leaves in eight weeks.

CARE / MAINTENANCE

Plants will run to seed if they dry out or lack food. Feed and water regularly if you want tender, succulent leaves.

PLANTING

12–15 plants should be sufficient for a 4–5 person family. Regularly replant to keep a continuous supply.

HARVESTING

Rather than cutting an entire plant, individual leaves can be picked much as one does with silver beet. Break off the leaf stalks cleanly with a quick downward action. Pick and cook directly, ensuring that all grit has been removed from the leaves.

PESTS AND DISEASES

Leaf miner and leaf spot, along with slugs and snails, will attack young seedlings. The miner can be treated with an insecticide, while leaf spot needs to be treated with a fungicide. Slugs and snails can either be removed by hand or a bait applied. Spinach that is grown quickly, kept moist and fed well is seldom attacked by pests and diseases.

IN POTS AND TUBS

Spinach will grow happily in containers. The handsome foliage is a bright green.

Sweet Corn

(Zea mays)

GROWING TIMES

Plant in full sun but in a spot sheltered from strong winds. The soil should be warm, so it pays to sow in late spring or early summer. It is also possible to sow well into summer in areas that have long autumns.

HEIGHT / SPREAD

Some varieties will grow as high as 3.5 m x 50 cm wide. Miniature types are available which grow to 1.5 m or less and 20–30 cm wide.

FROST HARDINESS

Not frost hardy.

SUN, SOIL, WATER, FOOD

Growing corn is relatively easy as long as your soil is rich and well dug over. These plants like plenty of food. Well made compost (and well decayed animal manure, if available) will encourage plants to grow fast and bear well. A suitable fertiliser mix is two parts of blood and bone to one part of superphosphate, or use a prepared general fertiliser at a rate of 100 g per square metre.

FLOWERS

Planting in blocks assists pollination. Shake the male flowers at the tops of the plants so that the pollen can drift down onto the female ears or silk, thereby ensuring a heavier crop.

GROWING FROM CUTTINGS OR SEED

Sow two or three seeds at the spaces recommended on the packets and later thin out the weakest, leaving the best seedling to grow.

CARE / MAINTENANCE

Plant in blocks so that the stems can be supported and tied together. Although corn will grow happily in quite dry conditions, regular watering will produce sweeter, succulent cobs more quickly.

PLANTING

20 plants will provide a reasonable crop for a family of four or five.

HARVESTING

Harvest when the silk turns brown and the cob swells. Feel the cob if you are unsure. It should feel plump and stand out from the stem. You can test the readiness of a cob by peeling back a little of the husk and pressing a thumb nail into a grain. If a milky fluid is exuded the cob is ready. Twist the cobs away from the stem without causing any damage and rush them inside to a pot of already boiling water. Fresh cobs are always sweetest.

PESTS AND DISEASES

Aphids, caterpillars (ear worm), and damping off all attack sweet corn. Treat with suitable sprays or use natural remedies such as soapy water and hand control of caterpillars. Dust seed with a fungicide before sowing to avoid damping off disease.

IN POTS AND TUBS

Miniature sweet corn makes an attractive pot plant, as does 'Indian Rainbow corn' (zea japonica). 'Japonica' grow to 2 m, 'Gracillima' to 130 cm. Corn grows well with beans, cucumber, marrow, melons, pumpkins, peas, potatoes and squash.

Tomato

(Lycopersicon Lysopersicum)

GROWING TIMES

Tomatoes need reliably warm weather to flourish and are best planted out as established plants in mid October. In warm northern areas they can be planted in early September and with a bit of luck they will be fruiting by Christmas.

HEIGHT / SPREAD

Varies with the variety chosen. Large types that need staking will grow to over 1.8 m and 50 cm or more wide. Small varieties like 'Microtom' grow only 12 cm tall and spread to 18 cm.

FROST HARDINESS

Very frost tender.

SUN, SOIL, WATER, FOOD

Tomatoes like full sun and a moist, well drained, rich soil mixed with plenty of compost. They resent lime and need phosphorus if they are to bear well. I starve my plants of both food and water until they produce their first set of flowers and then feed them with a weekly diet of liquid fertiliser and the occasional small handful of blood and bone or bone dust and superphosphate. Regular doses of liquid fertiliser also help boost the health and cropping capacity of plants. Mulching with compost or grass clippings also ensures a cool, moist root run and uninterrupted vigorous growth.

FLOWERS

Flowers are small and yellow, and not all that attractive to bees. Bee-attracting flowers planted near your tomatoes will ensure a better crop. Modern cultivars such as 'Oregon Spring' can set fruit without pollination and are very suitable for areas with a short growing season and cool summer nights.

GROWING FROM CUTTINGS OR SEED

Tomatoes are generally easy to grow from either seed or cuttings. Seeds can be sown directly into a warm, friable soil or into pots and transplanted out later when they are well established. In either case you should sow a few seeds in clumps and thin out all but the strongest.

CARE / MAINTENANCE

Hundreds of cultivars are now available which vary wildly in shape, size, flavour and colour. Training and the removing of side shoots depend on the type that you have chosen to grow. Many tall varieties need staking, tying and the side shoots removed regularly before they are more than 2–3 cm long. Dwarf and spreading varieties need no pruning or training.

PLANTING

Space standard tomatoes approximately 50 cm apart each way. 12 well grown tomato plants will be more than adequate for 4–5 people.

HARVESTING

Pick fruit every few days when it is evenly coloured and still firm. Leave to ripen for several days on a warm windowsill or place in a paper bag in a warm spot. Green tomatoes are perfectly edible and can be used in a variety of recipes. Tomatoes are also easy to pulp and freeze or simply freeze whole. They can then be added to winter soups and stews.

PESTS AND DISEASES

Thrips, whitefly, mite and caterpillars all affect tomatoes. Spray with a suitable insecticide or use organic sprays and remedies. Blossom drop is caused when spring temperatures drop very low or when they rise too high in the summer. Good ventilation will help solve summer temperature rises. Low spring temperatures can only be solved by carefully judging the best time to plant in your area. Fungal diseases are a major cause of tomato failure. Good soil preparation and adequate ventilation will help prevent fungal diseases. Vigorous varieties such as 'Mortgage Lifter' and 'Tommy Toe' are famous for their productivity and disease resistance.

IN POTS AND TUBS

Dwarf varieties are easy to grow in pots. Varieties such as 'Sweet 100s' and 'Microtoms' can be trained to climb or left to spill over the edge of a container.

Zucchini

(Curcubita Pepo)

GROWING TIMES

Annual – plant in the late spring, summer, and early autumn in warm areas.

HEIGHT / SPREAD

2 x 2 m. Some varieties are more compact. For zucchini varieties such as 'Black Beauty' or 'Costata Romanesco' you need only allow 1 m between plants. Many cultivars of curcubita pepo are available. What distinguishes them from other members of the pumpkin family is that they are harvested when the skin is tender and immature and are treated like a green vegetable.

FROST HARDINESS
Not frost hardy.

SUN, SOIL, WATER, FOOD
Sow or plant out container grown seedlings in full sun in a rich, fertile soil that has been enriched with copious quantities of well rotted compost and, if possible, well rotted animal manure. A highly nitrogenous fertiliser (NPK 10 / 4 / 6) applied when flowering commences will encourage a heavy crop. Liquid fertiliser applied at four to five weekly intervals will also boost yields. In hot weather a single plant can consume as much as ten litres of water a week. Don't overfeed plants as this can lead to leaves being produced at the expense of fruit.

FLOWERS
Poor fruit set can result if the weather is wet and bees are prevented from visiting the flowers. Fruit set is encouraged by hand pollination. The male flowers can be picked and the anthers rubbed on the stigma of the female ones. Female flowers are distinguished by a small swelling at the base of the flower that later develops into the fruit. The male flowers do not set fruit but are edible. They can be used in a variety of ways. 'Costata Romanesco' produces a heavy crop of male flowers.

GROWING FROM CUTTINGS OR SEED
Sow seeds in mounds only when the soil is warm. Sow at least four seeds to each mound (2 cm deep) and thin out when they have germinated, leaving only the strongest plant. Do not over-water. Plants will mature in 12–14 weeks after sowing. Dust seeds with a fungicide before sowing to prevent wilt and mildew developing.

CARE / MAINTENANCE
Once fruit has set water regularly and mulch plants with grass clippings. Planting through a layer of polythene (black plastic) or surrounding plants with a straw or compost mulch can also help preserve moisture in summer.

PLANTING
Six plants will produce sufficient zucchinis for the average family. After four weeks a second sowing can be made to ensure a succession of fruit throughout the growing season.

HARVESTING
Harvest when the fruit is 6–7 cm long and the skin tender. Regular picking encourages crop production.

PESTS AND DISEASES
Mildew and wilt are the most common diseases to affect all members of the curcubit family. Feed and water regularly so that plants are not subject to stress.

IN POTS AND TUBS
Compact growing varieties such as 'Black Beauty' will grow and bear well in pots if they are fed and watered regularly.

Dealing with Pests & Diseases

Controlling Insect Pests

Along with seasonal abundance in the vegetable garden, there comes a parallel increase in activity in the insect kingdom. If the problem is a minor one, you may take the position that we can spare a few morsels for the odd bug or bird. More serious infestations will require treatment if crops are to remain healthy. Listed below are both inorganic and organic remedies for common insect pests.

Aphids

Aphids cause plants to lose vigour and collapse. Shoots are stunted.

INORGANIC TREATMENT:	Systemic insecticides such as 'Mavrik' are very effective. Mavrik will kill insect pests yet will not harm the bees.
ORGANIC TREATMENT:	Ladybirds, waxeye (silvereye birds), parasitic wasps, and fungal diseases are good control agents. Soapy water, 'Neem Oil' Pyrethrum sprays or garlic spray are also effective. Watch carefully in the spring for the first signs of infestation.

Beetles (bronze, green etc.)

Beetles will strip plants of their leaves and devour flower buds.

INORGANIC TREATMENT:	Apply an insecticide spray.
ORGANIC TREATMENT:	Garlic sprays will deter them momentarily (see recipe on page 54). Shake them into a bucket of water that has a few drops of kerosene added. As a preventative, encourage plants to grow healthily and rapidly using foliar feeding.

Carrot rust fly

Young plants suffering from a carrot fly invasion will wilt, while older plants will show signs of burrowing.

INORGANIC TREATMENT:	Sprinkle Diazanon ('Soil Insect Killer') granules in the seed drill as sowing proceeds. Spray with Target.

ORGANIC TREATMENT:	Companion planting with onions, leeks, rosemary and sage will deter these pests. Use a succession of sowing dates so that some sowings will miss the peak egg laying flights of the carrot fly.

Caterpillars and leaf rollers

Caterpillars and leaf rollers will eat leaves and flower buds, and deposit droppings on leaves. Left to their own devices they can decimate a crop of cabbages.

INORGANIC TREATMENT:	Use an insecticide such as 'Mavrik', or Derris Dust with carbaryl added.
ORGANIC TREATMENT:	Remove by hand or dust with Derris Dust (or flour from the kitchen).

Cutworms

Cutworms shelter under plants during the day and come out to feed at night. Seedlings will suddenly fail, having had their stems eaten through.

INORGANIC TREATMENT:	Spray with a suitable insecticide.
ORGANIC TREATMENT:	Keep the soil free of weeds and apply an oak leaf mulch. Several parasitic wasps and tachinid flies may control cutworm larvae.

Mealy Bug

This pest has an oval body covered with white waxy threads. They are often found on indoor, balcony and greenhouse vegetables and ornamentals.

INORGANIC TREATMENT:	A systemic spray such as Orthene or 'Confidor'.
ORGANIC TREATMENT:	Wash the plant down outside with the hose. Use a soft brush dipped in a 50/50 methylated spirits and water mix to dislodge any determined bugs. Keep plants well-fed and healthy, and use a garlic spray.

Mite

Mites are tiny insects that attack young buds, causing them to contort and twist.

INORGANIC TREATMENT:	A miticide such as 'Mavrik' or 'Super Shield'.
ORGANIC TREATMENT:	Keep plants moist in the summer and spray the undersides of the leaves with water. Pick off and burn the first signs of this pest.

Red spider mite

These are tiny mites usually found on the undersides of leaves. They become bright red in the late summer and autumn, and flourish in hot dry conditions.

INORGANIC TREATMENT:	Use a miticide like 'Mavrik'.
ORGANIC TREATMENT:	Keep plants and the surrounding area sprayed with water. Pick off and destroy the first signs of this destructive pest.

Scale

Both hard and soft scale are rapid breeders. Both forms exude a sticky honeydew that attracts ants. A scale attack will debilitate and eventually kill a plant.

INORGANIC TREATMENT:	Apply an insecticide spray with a little horticultural oil added at summer strength.
ORGANIC TREATMENT:	Remove manually or use a toothbrush dipped in a weak solution of vinegar, oil and water.

Slaters

Slaters can do minor damage to crops.

INORGANIC TREATMENT:	Carbaryl will deter them but will kill earthworms.
ORGANIC TREATMENT:	Remove sheltering places such as rotting leaves. Regular cultivation of the soil will help.

The voracious snail.

Slugs and snails

Slugs and snails can do major damage to crops, and are especially hazardous to small seedlings. They are persistent and destructive garden pests.

INORGANIC TREATMENT:	'Mesurol' or similar bait.
ORGANIC TREATMENT:	'Quash' is a natural product and safe with animals. Crushed egg shells or sand placed around young seedlings will help protect them from slugs and snails. In severe cases trap them in stale beer in dishes, or in an upturned pot, or crush by hand and foot. Remove as much rotting vegetation as possible from the garden. This will eliminate breeding and hiding places.

Snail damage.

Sooty mould

Sooty mould is a tiny insect which feeds on the secretions of mealy bugs, scale and aphids. It appears on leaves as a dark soot-like mould, hence its name.

INORGANIC TREATMENT:	'Mavrik' with a little 'Conqueror Oil' added, or 'Orthene' or other general garden insecticide.
ORGANIC TREATMENT:	Garlic spray or soapy water.

Spittlebugs

Spittlebugs are common in spring and early summer. The insects form frothy bubbles that can be unsightly, but they do the garden little harm.

INORGANIC TREATMENT:	Hose the plants down first to get rid of the spittle froth, then spray with an insecticide like 'Mavrik'.
ORGANIC TREATMENT:	Regular hosings are often sufficient to keep the numbers down.

Thrips

Thrips are very small brown or black insects which feed on the sap of many plants. Foliage becomes silvery and dehydrated.

INORGANIC TREATMENT:	'Orthene', 'Gild' or Maldison.
ORGANIC TREATMENT:	Garlic spray. Keep plants healthy by regular, even feeding. Water regularly. Pick off and destroy any infected leaves as soon as the pest is seen.

Whitefly

Tiny, white and moth like. Unsightly and destructive sap sucking pest.

INORGANIC TREATMENT:	'Target' or 'Orthene'.
ORGANIC TREATMENT:	Garlic spray, 'Neem Oil' and regular sprayings with soapy water.

Garlic Spray

Garlic spray is a useful organic weapon against some insect pests. It is easy to make. You will need:

2 whole heads of garlic (approx 10 cloves each head)
1 teaspoon kerosene
1 litre of water
1 tablespoon of grated pure soap or Lux soap flakes

To prepare the spray:
Crush the garlic and mix with the kerosene. Boil the water with the soap flakes until they are dissolved. Cool, add the garlic and kerosene mixture, and strain. Keep this mixture in a sealed jar until you wish to use it. Dilute the mix at a ratio of 1 to 50 parts of water before applying to the garden. Omitting the garlic and substituting the boiled liquid from 12 rhubarb leaves can make a similar spray.

Treating Fungal Diseases

Much can be done to reduce the incidence of fungal disease by choosing disease-resistant plant varieties. Check the seed packets for information.

Blight

Blight appears on tomatoes and potatoes in warm, humid weather in mid to late summer. Leaves become distorted and the plant begins to fail.

INORGANIC TREATMENT:	Regular spraying with a copper based spray (such as 'Champion Copper') or a fungicide.
ORGANIC TREATMENT:	Use a garlic spray and remove any diseased leaves and burn them. Keep a free flow of air around plants by removing lower foliage in the case of tomatoes. Mulch with seaweed. Rotate crops and sprinkle a little lime under plants.

Damping off

This causes plants to sulk, refuse to grow, and then wilt and collapse at ground level.

INORGANIC TREATMENT:	A copper based spray, or 'Thiram'.
ORGANIC TREATMENT:	Avoid overwatering, use sterilised soil and keep a good airflow around plants.

Downy mildew

This mildew attacks cucumbers, leeks, lettuces, onions, peas, pumpkins, spinach and swede, especially when the weather is erratic.

INORGANIC TREATMENT:	Spray with a copper spray, 'Bravo' or 'Super Sulphur'.
ORGANIC TREATMENT:	Keep airflow circulating by removing excess foliage. Do not overcrowd when planting. Destroy affected area at the first signs of the disease. Use garlic spray.

Powdery mildew

Powdery mildew attacks when the soil is dry and the air is humid. The leaves and skins of cucumbers, marrows, melons, and pumpkins are covered in a white powdery coat. Even silver beet leaves can be affected.

INORGANIC TREATMENT:	Use a fungicide spray such as 'Bravo', 'Saprol', 'Green Guard' or 'Yates Fungus Fighter'.

ORGANIC TREATMENT: Space plants so that the air can move freely. Rotate crops. Keep the soil moist during dry periods. A spray made of a weak vinegar solution helps. Flowers of sulphur sprinkled on the leaves is also useful.

Rust

Rust is a difficult disease to control. It can destroy crops of beetroot, broad beans, garlic and leeks. Brownish orange spores form on infected plants.

INORGANIC TREATMENT: Copper sprays or weekly sprayings of 'Saprol'.

ORGANIC TREATMENT: Remove and burn all infected leaves as soon as they appear. Mulch the soil heavily with sawdust or seaweed. Rotate crops to prevent re-infection. Avoid using heavily nitrogenous fertiliser. Use rust resistant seed.

Organic Anti-Fungal Spray

To form a base add 2.5 tablespoons of horticultural oil to 4.5 litres of water. (Horticultural oil is available from garden centres.) Then add the following:

1 tablespoon of Palmolive liquid soap. This helps the spray adhere to the plants.

1 tablespoon of fish emulsion (Alaska or similar). This discourages insects and also feeds the plants.

1 tablespoon of baking soda. This controls fungal diseases such as mildew.

2 drops of Nitrosol or other liquid fertiliser. This feeds the plants and boosts their immunity to disease.

Wash the vegetable garden well with the hose in the morning, prior to spraying with this mixture in the evening. Allow the leaves to dry before spraying. This spray will also help deter insects.

Monthly Gardening Guide

Ensuring a succession of vegetables

In a small garden it can be difficult to produce vegetables in succession throughout the year. While radishes and lettuce can be sown every third week in small quantities and thinned out, other vegetables are not so easy to regulate. The easiest way to solve the problem is to raise young seedlings in trays and peat pots and plant them out as soon as the previous crop finishes, or to practise inter-cropping. While this doesn't produce a seamless supply, it does limit the time between crops considerably.

SPRING

September

- Sow seeds of artichoke (globe), asparagus, beetroot, bok choy, broad beans, cabbage, cauliflower, celery, corn salad, courgette (zucchini), onions, parsnip, peas, radish, spinach, silver beet, swede, tomato and turnip.
- Protect zucchini, capsicum and tomato seedlings from late frosts.

October

- Sow seeds of bok choy, climbing and dwarf beans, beetroot, Brussels sprouts, cabbage, capsicum, carrot, cauliflower, celery, corn salad, cucumber (in warm areas), leeks, marrows, New Zealand spinach, spring onions, silver beet, swede, sweet corn, turnip and tomato.
- In warm areas you can also plant main crop potato sets and kumara.

November

- In mild areas plant or sow pumpkin, radish, squash, spring onions, silver beet, swede, sweet corn, tomato, turnip and zucchini.
- In cooler areas sow seeds or plant seedlings of bok choy, dwarf and climbing beans, broccoli, Brussels sprouts, cabbage, carrot, cauliflower, celery, chicory, corn salad, cucumber, Florence fennel, leeks, lettuce, parsnip and peas.

SUMMER

December

- In warmer gardens sow or plant seedlings of the following: bok choy, dwarf and climbing beans, beetroot, sprouting broccoli, Brussels sprouts, cabbage, carrot, cauliflower, capsicum, Florence fennel, leeks, lettuce, zucchini, melons, parsley, spinach, parsnip, peas.
- In cooler gardens plant pumpkin, squash, silver beet, sweet corn, turnip, tomato and zucchini.

January

- Sow or plant seedlings of dwarf and climbing beans, beetroot, bok choy, broccoli (both heading and sprouting), Brussels sprouts, cabbage, carrot, cauliflower, celery, corn salad, cucumber, Florence fennel, parsley, kale, leek, lettuce, zucchini.
- Melons, zucchini, squash and pumpkin need at least 180 days before the first frost if they are to ripen.
- In mild northern areas there is still time to plant or sow turnip, tomatoes and zucchini.
- In cool areas sow or plant silver beet, swede and sweet corn.

February

- In many southern areas it is best to plan for autumn and plant cooler season vegetables. Even in the warmer north it is best to begin planning the winter garden.
- Beetroot, broccoli, Brussels sprouts, cabbage, carrot, cauliflower, chicory, corn salad, kale, leek, and lettuce can be planted in most gardens.
- In warm areas sow seeds of bok choy, dwarf and climbing beans.
- In cool areas plant swede and turnip.
- Peas, potatoes, radish, silver beet and spinach should only be planted where they are not endangered by heavy frosts.

AUTUMN

March

- Dry, hot weather is the rule in most parts of the country. Seeds of some vegetables can be sown, but in many areas it may be better to wait until spring.
- In mild areas plant seedlings of cauliflower, chicory and corn, and set out potatoes.
- In areas not subject to constant winter frost you can plant beetroot, broccoli, Brussels sprouts, cabbage, carrot and parsley.
- In areas where the winters are frosty plant swede and turnip.

April

- Plant seedlings of broad beans, beetroot, broccoli, cabbage, cauliflower, corn salad, lettuce, onions and parsley.
- In warm gardens plant leeks and turnip.

May

- If the soil is reasonably warm you can plant seedlings of the following: cabbage, cauliflower, corn salad, onions, peas, radish, silver beet, spinach and turnip. Shallots and garlic can also be planted.
- If local conditions are already cold, leave planting until the spring.

WINTER

June

- If conditions are suitable you can plant broad beans, cabbage, corn salad, peas, spinach, cauliflower, celery, lettuce, silver beet and turnips.
- If conditions are not suitable sow in trays for early spring planting, or simply wait until the weather warms.

July

- Where the soil is warm, light and well drained you can sow seeds of corn salad, onions, peas, lettuce, silver beet, spinach, cabbage and cauliflower.
- Seedlings of the above (including celery) can be planted out, as can shallots, garlic and well sprouted potatoes.

August

- If your soil is warm and friable sow seeds of beetroot, broad beans, cabbage, carrot, cauliflower, corn salad, leeks, lettuce, onions, parsnips, peas, silver beet, spinach and turnip.
- Asparagus seedlings can be planted out in northern areas. In the south it is better to wait a month or so.

Vegetables – Spacing, Storage & Yield

VEGETABLE	BETWEEN ROWS	BETWEEN PLANTS
Asparagus	60 cm	30 cm
Aubergine	75 cm	60 cm
Beans (Broad)	45 cm	10 cm
Beans (Runner)	60 cm	8–10 cm
Beetroot	30 cm	10–14 cm
Bok Choy	30 cm	20 cm
Broccoli	50–75 cm	50–70 cm
Cabbage	50 cm	35–45 cm
Capsicum	50 cm	50–60 cm
Carrot	15–20 cm	10 cm
Celery	40 cm	40 cm
Chicory	30 cm	30 cm
Cucumber	60 cm	40 cm
Garlic	40–50 cm	15–20 cm
Leek	40 cm	15–20 cm
Lettuce	30 cm	30 cm
Mustard (Giant Red)	40 cm	40–50 cm
Peas	12 cm [1]	12 cm
Potato	60 cm	30–40 cm
Pumpkin	1 m	1 m
Silver Beet	35–40 cm	30 cm
Spinach	30 cm	20 cm
Sweet Corn	35 cm	35 cm
Tomato	40–45 cm	40 cm
Zucchini (Courgettes)	90 cm	90 cm

1. Peas are best planted in triple rows with seeds 12 cm apart each way.

STORAGE	YIELD PER 1 METRE ROW
Best fresh	2 kg
Eat fresh	6–10 fruit
Freezes well	3.5 kg
Freezes well	7 kg
Stores well	3 kg
Eat fresh	5–6 plants
Freezes well	2–3 kgs
Eat fresh	6–8 heads
Freezes well	6–10 fruit
Stores well	3.5 kg
Eat fresh	2–3plants
Eat fresh	3–4 heads
Best fresh	10–12 fruits per plant
Stores well	7–8 heads
Best fresh	2.5 kg
Best fresh	3–4 heads
Stores well	3–4 kg
Freezes well	2.5–3 kg
Stores well	2–3 kg
Stores well	20 kg +
Best fresh	3 kg
Freezes well	2.5 kg
Freezes well	3–4 cobs
Freezes well	3.5 kg
Best fresh	2 kg

Water Requirements

VEGETABLE	WHEN TO WATER
Asparagus	Never
Aubergine	When fruit is developing
Beans (Broad)	Flowering time & pod swell
Beans (Runner)	Throughout growth
Beetroot	Just before planting
Bok Choy	Puddle in at planting & water throughout growth
Broccoli	Puddle in at planting
Cabbage	Puddle in at planting
Capsicum	At planting and as crop forms
Carrot	Never
Celery	Throughout growth
Chicory	Throughout growth
Cucumber	Throughout growth
Garlic	When planting (sparingly while growing)
Leek	Throughout growth
Lettuce	Throughout growth
Mustard (Giant Red)	Throughout growth
Peas	At sowing, flowering & pod swell
Potato (early)	Throughout growth
Potato (main crop)	When flowers appear
Pumpkin	When fruit begins to swell
Silver Beet	Puddle in at planting & keep soil evenly moist
Spinach	Throughout growth
Sweet Corn	At planting & as cobs swell
Tomato	Regularly, once flowers are set
Zucchini (Courgettes)	When fruit begins to swell

WHY

Water is stored in plants from winter rains

Healthier crop

Better yield

More flowers, better bean size & quantity

Establishes plants

Quick growth is essential

Establishes plants

Establishes plants

Juicier fruit

Will produce foliage at the expense of roots

Likes copious water

Quicker growth & juicier crops

Quicker growth & juicier crops

Too much water causes root rot

Bigger stems & leaves

Bigger size, more succulent crop

Larger leaves

Increases cropping

Earlier cropping

Larger crop

Larger fruit

Any check in growth or sudden change
in conditions can lead to bolting (going to seed)

Encourages crisp foliage & stems

Aids growth and cob juiciness

Take care – excess moisture decreases flavour

Water increases cropping